Lionel Train

FIELD GUIDE
1945-1969

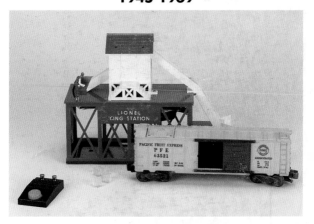

David Doyle

Values and Identification

©2006 David Doyle
Published by

kp krause publications
An Imprint of F+W Publications

700 East State Street • Iola, WI 54990-0001
715-445-2214 • 888-457-2873

Library of Congress Catalog Number: 2005906845

ISBN 10-digit: 0-89689-299-9
ISBN 13-digit: 978-0-89689-299-6

Designed by Wendy Wendt
Edited by Dennis Thornton

Printed in China

Acknowledgments

A book of this nature would be impossible to compile without the generous help of many individuals and friends. While I put this together, many collectors and businesses shared photographs with me or allowed me to make my own images of rare and important pieces in their collections. Many knowledgeable collectors and dealers graciously reviewed the manuscript and offered corrections, criticism and commentary, and provided valuable insight on values for the items listed herein. Every effort has been made to present complete and accurate information here, and any errors are purely my own.

Former TCA presidents Dr. Paul Wassermann and Gordon Wilson supplied additional images for that, and other chapters as well.

Parts with Character shared much knowledge and experience with me, as well as allowing needed photos to be taken.

My old friend, Jeff Kane of www.ttender.com, sent needed photos of many individual items.

Train collecting is a passion for the entire Tschopp family, and they all pitched in on this project. Brothers Bob and John opened their collection for photography and shared their knowledge, and teen-ager Bobby, the newest collector of the family, tirelessly located trains for photography.

Greg Stout of Stout Auctions, who arguably handles the largest train collections in the country, granted us unlimited access for photography and, as a result, saved many, many hours of work and miles of driving. His phenomenal knowledge and amazing memory were tremendous assets in this project.

Vince Trimarco was kind enough to photograph several items from his collection of Lionel HO for this volume.

A handful of collectors chose to remain anonymous. Their anonymity, however, does not lessen the value of their contributions of photographs and information to this work—thank you.

Warman's Lionel Train Field Guide

Contents

How to Use This Field Guide

This book is intended to aid both the novice and the experienced collector of Lionel products. It is a pocket-sized version of The Standard Catalog of Lionel Trains 1945-1969, easy to take to shows as both a checklist and price guide. Though lacking the detail of the full-sized version, enough information is provided to differentiate between not only the primary collectible variations, but also a number of the often-forged items and authentic pieces.

This book is broken down into the following sections: Locomotives and Rolling Stock, Accessories, Cataloged Sets and Catalogs. Within these sections, the items are arranged numerically by stock number. The stock number on the vast majority of Lionel's products was stamped either on the side or underside of the item. The items are listed in numeric order in each chapter. The variations of each item are presented in chronological order, if known, or in increasing order of scarcity if the production sequence is unknown.

Thus, if you pick up a flatcar that is numbered 6467, you can turn to the flatcar section and move through the listings until you reach the number 6467. You will then find that this car was produced only in 1956, and was cataloged by Lionel as a "Miscellaneous Car." Nearby most listings, you will find a photo of the item described.

For items produced over a period of years, several details must be studied to accurately date each piece. Most of these dating clues involve the trucks and couplers on the cars, or boxes they were packaged in. These changes are detailed here, and a summary of these changes appears at the bottom of each page throughout the listings.

Lionel trains were built to provide a "lifetime of happiness," to quote the vintage advertising slogan, and with proper care they will do that and more. Resist the temptation to simply pull them from the attic and put them on the track or grab the first household cleanser you find to clean them with. Either of these things could cause permanent, costly damage to an otherwise fine collectible and toy.

Condition and Rarity

To the collector, condition is everything, and the Train Collectors Association, the world's oldest and largest train collector group, has established very precise language for describing the condition of collectible trains to protect both the buyer and the seller. All reputable dealers and collectors use this terminology and, in fact, failure to properly use these terms in transactions between members can result in expulsion from the organization.

These grading standards are as follows:

Fair: Well-scratched, chipped, dented, rusted, warped.

Good: Small dents, scratches, dirty.

Very Good: Few scratches, exceptionally clean, no major dents or rust.

Excellent: Minute scratches or nicks, no dents or rust, all original, less than average wear.

Like New: Only the slightest signs of handling and wheel wear, brilliant colors and crisp markings; literally like new. As a rule, Like New trains must have their original boxes in comparable condition to realize the prices listed in the guide.

Mint: Brand new, absolutely unmarred, all original and unused. Items dusty or faded from display, or with fingerprints from handling, cannot be considered mint. Although Lionel test ran their locomotives briefly at the factory, items "test run" by consumers cannot be considered mint. Most collectors expect mint items to come with all associated packaging with which they were originally supplied.

As one can imagine, Mint pieces command premium prices. The supply is extremely limited, and the demand among collectors is great, so often the billfold of the buyer, rather than a more natural supply and demand situation, limits the price of such pieces.

Demand is one of the key factors influencing values. The Santa Fe F-3 diesel was the most produced locomotive in Lionel's history, yet clean examples still command premium prices due to demand. Its classic beauty endures and essentially every enthusiast or layperson wants one.

Scarcity or rarity, or, is also a factor influencing the value of trains. Low production quantities or extreme fragility cause some items to be substantially more difficult to find than others. When scarcity is coupled with demand, the result is a premium price. Other items, extremely scarce, command only moderate prices due to lack of demand, or appreciation, on the part of collectors. In this guide we have rated each item on a scale of one to eight for rarity. One represents the most common items, such as the 6017 caboose, while eight is assigned to those items hardest to find, such as the gray 3562-1 barrel car with red lettering. It is hoped that this rarity rating will help the collector when having to choose which similar priced items to buy by answering the proverbial "how likely am I to get this chance again?" question.

Supply, as a short-term extension of rarity, whether actual or temporary, also affects price. If only one sought after item is at a given show, the seller is unlikely to negotiate or reduce his price. If, however, multiple sellers at a given event have identical items, no matter how rare, the temporary market glut can bring about temporarily reduced prices.

Lastly, the **buyer's intent** will affect what they are willing to pay. A collector, who intends to add a piece to his or her permanent collection, will obviously pay more for an item than a dealer who is intending to resell the item will pay for the same item.

Prices are given in this guide for trains in Very Good, Excellent and Like New condition. Trains in less than Very Good condition are not generally considered collectible, and, as mentioned earlier, Mint condition trains are too uncommon to establish pricing.

The prices listed are what a group of collectors would consider a reasonable price to pay to add that piece to their collections. When contemplating a sale to a dealer, you should expect to receive 30 percent to 50 percent less than the listed values, with the poorer condition the trains the greater the amount of discount, due to the greater difficulty the dealer will have selling them. Remember that these prices are only a guideline. You are spending your money. What an item is worth to you is of greater importance than what it is worth to the author. Conversely, the publisher does not sell trains, this is not a mail-order catalog, and you should not expect a dealer or collector to "price match."

Aids to Dating Trains

Unlike certain other collectibles, the age of a Lionel train is not a factor in its value. That is, an older train is not inherently more valuable than a newer train. It is rather the variations in construction throughout an item's production run that affect its scarcity, and thus value. Many Lionel trains are marked on the sides with "New" or "Built" dates. These dates are totally irrelevant to when a piece was actually produced, and are decorative only. During the mid-1950s, Lionel added the year introduced as a prefix or suffix to the stock number of some cars, such as the 336155 markings on the log dump cars introduced in 1955, or the 546446 N & W hopper car from 1954, but this was not universally done.

Although a few collectors specialize in a specific year or two of Lionel production, they are the exception. Rather, the establishing the production date of these trains is done more as a curiosity by most collectors, or when trying to properly and precisely recreate a given train set.

Among the key aids to dating trains are the construction techniques used in the manufacture of the trucks and couplers, and the type of original packaging used, if still present.

Lionel Freight Trucks

The trucks that collectors refer to as **"staple-end"** are so named because the end of the bolster (the upper crosspiece of a truck, which serves as its attachment point to the railroad car) has been staked to secure the zinc sideframes. The staking resembles a folded staple, thus the moniker.

These so-called staple end trucks were used from 1945 until 1951.

In 1951, the staple end trucks were superceded by what collectors refer to as **"bar-end"** trucks. The earlier design allowed, with time, the sideframes to loosen from the bolster. The improved design featured the sideframes being forced down onto the bolster. Thus, the end of the bolster visible to the observer remains smooth, and looks like a steel bar. This truck was the mainstay of Lionel's freight car production until 1961, when it was largely phased out until 1969, when it reappeared on selected better items.

The **"Scout"** truck was introduced in 1948, along with its associated coupler, as a low-cost component of these low-cost sets. The bolster and side frame supports were a single piece of stamped steel, with the sideframes being separate pieces of plastic attached to the sheet metal. While the scout coupler was discontinued in 1951 because it was incompatible with the normal Lionel coupler, the truck itself lingered until 1953 before being phased out, being equipped in its twilight years with standard magnetic couplers.

In 1957, Lionel introduced their new plastic truck. Molded of Delrin, a self-lubricating plastic, the detailed trucks were styled after a real railroad truck developed by the Association of American Railroads **(AAR)**, and bore the tiny raised word **"Timken"** on the ends of the simulated journals.

Archbar trucks were introduced in 1959 to equip the new line of 19th Century style trains pulled by the "General" steam locomotive inspired by Disney's "Great Locomotive Chase" movie. These trucks, like the AAR trucks, were molded plastic and, though very different cosmetically from the AAR-trucks, were almost identical from the manufacturing standpoint.

Lionel Boxes

The box that most often comes to the mind's eye when thinking about Lionel trains is the traditional orange and blue box. However, from 1945 through 1969, Lionel used no less than 15 types of boxes for its rolling stock. The changes in the boxes can be an aid to dating trains that are known to be in their original packages, such as those purchased from their original owner or found in an attic. Beware, however, that many unknowing (or uncaring) collectors and dealers often place items in the improper vintage box in an effort to "upgrade" the packaging.

EARLY POSTWAR: The original boxes used for individual cars and small accessories in the postwar era had bold blue lettering that touched the tops and bottoms of the blue lettering frames and outlines. This box was used from 1945 through 1947; the 1947 boxes are distinguished by the logo of the Toy Manufacturers Association.

FIRST TRADITIONAL: The most remembered box of the postwar era was introduced in 1948. The names of cities with Lionel showrooms—"NEW YORK," "CHICAGO" and "SAN FRANCISCO"—were imprinted inside borders on the sides of the box. The stock number of the box contents was printed on all four sides of the box, as well as on the end flaps.

MIDDLE TRADITIONAL: This box is the same as Early Traditional, except the city name "SAN FRANCISCO" was eliminated, reflecting the closure of the West Coast sales office. This box was in use from mid-1949 through 1955. However, the 1955 boxes were considerably redesigned. The heavy corrugated cardboard liners that previously had been used inside of many of the boxes, particularly locomotives, were eliminated, and the boxes downsized accordingly.

OPS TRADITIONAL: This box was the same as the Middle Traditional, but was factory printed with a Korean War-era OPS (Office of Price Stabilization) price. This box was used in 1952. As an aside, Lionel provided dealers with sheets of adhesive-backed white OPS stickers for application to older items already in stock.

LATE TRADITIONAL: This box is the same as the Middle Traditional, except for the removal of the stock number from the four sides, leaving it only on the ends. This box was introduced in 1956 and used through 1958.

BOLD TRADITIONAL: The Bold Traditional box is an uncommon box similar to the Late Traditional box, but had much bolder typeface print on the end flaps. This box was only used during 1958, and then only for part of the product line.

GLOSSY: In 1958, a few boxes were made of smooth, glossy coated cardstock. This box is very uncommon.

PERFORATED: By 1959, merchandising trends had moved toward consumer self-service and Lionel's products had an increasing presence in discount chains. This resulted in a total change in Lionel's packaging. The new box was made of orange-coated stock and featured a tear-out perforated front panel that allowed the contents to be displayed. This box was introduced in 1959 and used through 1960.

ORANGE PICTURE: This box, also made of glossy orange cardstock, had a white panel with an illustration of a steam and diesel locomotive on the front. The city names

"NEW YORK" and "CHICAGO" appeared on the box, as did the corporate name "THE LIONEL CORPORATION." This is the box that was in use from 1961 through 1964.

PERFORATED PICTURE: During 1961 and 1962, boxes were occasionally produced that featured an illustrated white front panel, which also was perforated for removal.

HILLSIDE PICTURE: This was essentially the same as the Orange Picture, but rather than the showroom locations of New York and Chicago, the box sides bore "HILLSIDE, N.J.," (the location of Lionel's factory) and bore the new corporate name "THE LIONEL TOY CORPORATION." This box was used for part of the 1965.

WINDOW BOX: Furthering the idea introduced with 1958's perforated box, in 1966, Lionel introduced the window box. With this box, the contents were still visible through a cellophane window in the front of the box, but were protected from shop wear and dust. Today this box is often found with cellophane loose or missing. The boxes were more generic than their predecessors, with the stock number being rubber-stamped according to contents, rather than being machine printed during the box's manufacturing process.

HAGERSTOWN CHECKERBOARD: In 1968, the boxes were revised yet again. Now the boxes featured a bold white and orange checkerboard pattern. Yet again, the city imprint changed as well, this time to "HAGERSTOWN, MARYLAND," reflecting Lionel's 1967 relocation of manufacturing operations the Hagerstown facility of its Porter science subsidiary. Unlike the custom packaging of the 1950s, one size of Checkerboard box was used for the vast majority of the rolling stock. In most cases, the stock numbers were rubber-stamped on boxes.

HILLSIDE CHECKERBOARD: Lionel returned to Hillside, N.J., in 1969, and the boxes reflected the move. Other than the city imprint, the Hillside Checkerboard boxes were the same as the Checkerboard.

GENERIC: During the final days of the postwar era, from time to time Lionel resorted to using plain white boxes with stock numbers rubber-stamped, or occasionally type-stamped on the end flaps.

Lionel Trains and the Collecting Hobby

Lionel. Few brand names have the instantaneous recognition that Lionel enjoys as it enters its second century. Young or old, male or female, it seems almost everyone identifies the name with toy trains—in fact, to many people the two are synonymous.

Joshua Lionel Cohen, with Harry Grant, formed the firm on Sept. 5, 1900. Their first business was with the U.S. Navy, producing fuses for mines. Once the Navy work was completed, Cohen began tinkering, trying to find a product to keep he and his partner busy and his new firm afloat. Adapting a motor Lionel developed for a fan, they created a motorized gondola car. Provided with a circle of steel rails, it was intended as an animated store window display. The year was 1901 and this was the first Lionel Electric Train.

World War II brought a halt to Lionel's toy train production in June 1942. The Lionel plant, like countless others throughout the country, became totally devoted to manufacturing military products. World War II also brought other changes to Lionel's operations, as large numbers of women joined the workforce. The complete cessation of train production for three years provided Lionel the opportunity to complete revamp its line. When production resumed in the fall of 1945, not only was Standard Gauge not mentioned, but the 0-gauge trains had totally new designed trucks and couplers, which were incompatible with the previous models, and a newly designed plastic-bodied gondola car. Over the next few years, plastics would increasingly replace the previously used metals in Lionel's products.

The late 1940s and 1950s were Lionel's glory years, with the Irvington plant churning out thousands of trains in dozens of models and hundreds of paint schemes.

Some of the features Lionel Trains are known for were introduced prior to World War II: die-cast boilers, electrical reversing mechanisms (dubbed "E-units") and the whistle all predate World War II. However, the postwar era brought about many more innovations. "Real railroad knuckle couplers" debuted in 1945, the next year smoke was added to many steam locomotives, America's favorite milk man first unloaded the milk car in 1947, the famed Santa Fe F3 streamlined diesel took to Lionel's rails in 1948 and, though untouted until 1950, in 1949 Lionel introduced Magnetraction, which magnetized the wheels of locomotives.

Ultimately, in 1969, the Lionel Toy Corporation (as it had become in 1965) exited the toy train business by licensing the name and selling the tooling to the Fundimensions

Division of General Mills. Some production was moved immediately and, by the mid-1970s, Lionel trains were no longer a presence in the huge Hillside plant.

With the exception of 1967, Lionel Trains have been, and are still, in production every year since 1945. Today's Lionel trains have elaborate paint schemes and sophisticated electronics undreamed of during the postwar heyday.

Collecting Groups

Toy train collectors are their own fraternity, eagerly welcoming new buffs with a sincere interest in toy trains. Avail yourself of this knowledge base and friendship. No matter if you are an experienced collector or a rookie, something can always be learned. There is no substitute for experience in this hobby, as in any other. No book, no matter how complete, contains all the answers. Thousands of words and the best illustrations cannot equal the experience gained by holding a piece in your own hands. There is no finer place than in the home of a friend and fellow collector. The piece that is not for sale can be examined unhurried and questions can be answered honestly; an excellent preparation for seeking an item in the marketplace.

The advent of Internet auctions has been a boon for collectors in remote areas. But for those in more populous areas, there is no substitute for shopping in the company of fellow collectors in hobby shops and train shows. Examining an item personally, with the counsel of more experienced collectors, is especially urged when purchasing expensive, repaired or forged items.

Enthusiasts have been collecting toy trains perhaps as long as they have been being produced. In the United States, the largest and oldest collectors group is the Train Collectors Association (TCA). Founded in 1954 in Yardley, Pa., the group has grown to more than 31,000 members. The nationally recognized Grading Standards used in this volume were developed by the TCA.

The TCA headquarters is located in its Toy Train Museum and can be reached at:

The Train Collectors Association
P.O. Box 248
300 Paradise Lane
Strasburg, PA 17579
Phone (717) 687-8623

The second-oldest organization is the Toy Train Operating Society, formed on the West Coast in 1966. The TTOS can be contacted at:

Toy Train Operating Society
25 W. Walnut Street, Suite 308
Pasadena, CA 91103
Phone (626) 578-0673

The largest Lionel-specific club is the Lionel Collector's Club of America. The club's mailing address is:

LCCA Business Office
P.O. Box 479
La Salle, IL 61301-0479

The purpose of the Lionel Operating Train Society, or LOTS, is to providing a national club for operators (as opposed to pure collectors) of Lionel trains and accessories. LOTS can be reached at:

LOTS Business Office
6376 West Fork Road
Cincinnati, OH 45247-5704

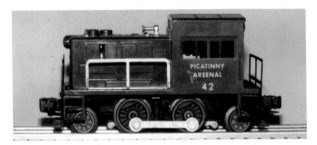

42 Picatinny Arsenal Switcher

51 Navy Yard New York Switcher

Locomotives and Rolling Stock

Locomotives and rolling stock present the largest category of collectible Lionel trains—fitting, as these are the trains themselves. Listed here in numeric order is the postwar production of these items, and their key variations.

#	Description	VG	EX	LN	S
41 UNITED STATES ARMY SWITCHER: 1955-57, painted		125	160	200	3
unpainted, black body		200	300	400	5
42 PICATINNY ARSENAL SWITCHER: 1957 unpainted olive drab body		200	300	400	5
44 U.S. ARMY MOBILE MISSILE LAUNCHER: 1959-62, painted blue body		150	225	350	5
45 U.S. MARINES MOBILE MISSILE LAUNCHER: 1960-62, painted olive drab		175	275	425	6
50 LIONEL GANG CAR: 1954-64. Gray bumpers (1954) two-piece horn		375	500	675	7
Blue bumpers, two-piece horn		50	75	125	4
Blue bumpers, one-piece horn		40	60	75	2
51 NAVY YARD NEW YORK SWITCHER: 1956-57, unpainted blue plastic body		125	175	250	4

56 M St L Switcher

58 Great Northern Switcher/Snowplow

#	Description	VG	EX	LN	S
52 FIRE CAR: 1958-61, red-painted black plastic body		125	200	300	5
53 RIO GRANDE SWITCHER: 1957-60. With plow "a" in Rio Grande printed normally....		425	600	900	8
"A" in Rio Grande reversed (prototypically correct)		225	325	450	6
54 BALLAST TAMPER: 1958-61, 1966-69, unpainted yellow plastic body		150	225	325	5
55 TIE-JECTOR: 1957-61		150	225	325	5
56 M St L SWITCHER: 1958, body painted red, cab sides painted white		300	550	800	6
57 AEC SWITCHER: 1959-60, unpainted white body, cab sides painted red		450	700	1200	7
58 GREAT NORTHERN SWITCHER/ SNOWPLOW: 1959-1961 unpainted green plastic, with white cab sides equipped with a rotary snow blower		300	500	800	5
59 U.S. AIR FORCE MINUTEMAN SWITCHER: 1961-63, unpainted white body		300	500	750	5

60 Lionelville Rapid Transit Trolley

69 Maintenance Car

#	Description	VG	EX	LN	S
60 LIONELVILLE RAPID TRANSIT TROLLEY: 1955-58, yellow body, red roof.					
	Black lettering, no vents, metal motorman silhouettes	200	300	400	5
	Black lettering, no vents, no motorman silhouettes	150	275	350	4
	Blue lettering, no vents, no motormen	100	175	250	3
	Blue lettering, no motormen, with vents	150	225	325	4
65 HANDCAR: 1962-66, molded.					
	Light yellow plastic body	200	400	600	5
	Dark yellow plastic body	175	325	500	4
	Strengthened body molding.	225	450	650	6
68 EXECUTIVE INSPECTION CAR: 1958-61, gray plastic, painted red and cream	175	300	425	4
69 MAINTENANCE CAR: 1960-62, dark gray brushplate, black body, both unpainted	225	350	500	5
202 UNION PACIFIC ALCO A: 1957 painted orange	75	100	150	2
204 SANTA FE ALCO A-A: 1957 powered and dummy painted blue and yellow. Dummy has operating headlight	100	175	275	4

208 Santa Fe Alco A-A

209 New Haven Alco A-A

210 Texas Special Alco A-A

212 United States Marine Corps Alco A

#	Description	VG	EX	LN	S
205 MISSOURI PACIFIC ALCO A-A: 1957-58, painted solid blue.					
With factory installed steel nose supports . . .		100	175	275	5
Without factory installed steel nose supports painted to match		75	150	250	4
208 SANTA FE ALCO A-A: 1958-59 painted blue and yellow, no headlight in dummy		75	150	250	4
209 NEW HAVEN ALCO A-A: 1958 only, black, white and orange paint on molded black plastic body		400	600	1000	6
210 TEXAS SPECIAL ALCO A-A: 1958 only, painted red and white body.		75	150	250	4
211 TEXAS SPECIAL ALCO A-A: 1962-63, 1965-66, cosmetically almost identical to the 210 . .		75	150	250	5
212 SANTA FE ALCO A-A: 1964-66, painted red and silver. Some stamped "BLT / BY LIONEL". Others were stamped "BLT 8-57 / BY LIONEL", but no difference in value or scarcity		100	175	275	4
212 UNITED STATES MARINE CORPS ALCO A: 1958-59.					
Painted dark blue		100	175	250	4
Painted medium blue		150	225	325	6

212(T) United States Marine Corps Alco A Dummy

213 Minneapolis & St. Louis Alco A-A

216 Burlington Alco A

#	Description	VG	EX	LN	S
212(T) UNITED STATES MARINE CORPS ALCO A dummy: 1958, painted medium blue body		450	675	1100	7
213 MINNEAPOLIS & ST. LOUIS ALCO A-A: 1964, painted red		125	225	325	5
215 SANTA FE ALCO: 1965-66, painted red and silver.					
A-A with 212T		100.	150	250	3
A-B with 218C		110.	175	275	4
216 BURLINGTON ALCO A: 1958 painted silver and red..............................		200	350	450	6
216 MINNEAPOLIS & ST. LOUIS ALCO A: 1965.					
Painted red body, came as single A unit.....		100	150	200	4
A-A combination with 213		175	225	350	5
217 B & M ALCO A-B: 1959, unpainted blue plastic bodies with the roof and A-unit nose painted black		100	165	250	5
218 SANTA FE ALCO: 1959-63 painted silver and red.					
A-A, normal nose decal.................		100	150	225	3
A-A solid yellow nose decals that lacked the red areas inside the perimeter		125	175	275	5
A-B combination (1961)...............		100	150	250	4

2-6-4 Steam

221 Rio Grande Alco A

221 Santa Fe Alco A

#	Description	VG	EX	LN	S
218 C SANTA FE ALCO B UNIT: 1961-63, painted silver		50	75	115	4
219 MISSOURI PACIFIC ALCO A-A: 1959 only uncataloged blue-painted pair		100	175	290	5
220 SANTA FE ALCO: 1960-61, painted silver and red, A only		75	125	175	3
A-A combination		150	225	300	3
221 2-6-4 STEAM: 1946-47, painted either 221T or 221W tender.					
Gray, silver wheels		100	150	200	4
Gray, black wheels		75	100	150	3
Black, black wheels		50	75	125	2
221 RIO GRANDE ALCO A: 1963-64, unpainted yellow body		50	70	90	2
221 SANTA FE ALCO A: 1964, uncataloged, unpainted olive drab body, no E-unit, wired for forward-only travel		250	500	750	7
221 UNITED STATES MARINE CORPS ALCO A: 1964, uncataloged, unpainted olive drab body.		225	375	550	6
222 RIO GRANDE ALCO A: 1962, painted yellow, wired to run forward only		50	75	100	2

224 United States Navy Alco A-B

225 Chesapeake & Ohio Alco A

226 B & M Alco A-B

229 Minneapolis & St. Louis Alco

# Description	VG	EX	LN	S
223 SANTA FE ALCO A-B: 1963, Painted silver and red	125	200	325	5
224 2-6-2 STEAM: 1945-46, with 2466W or 2466WX tender. 1945, without tender drawbar, black railings, squared cab floor	75	125	200	4
1946, with tender drawbar, silver railings, rounded cab floor	60	100	150	2
224 UNITED STATES NAVY ALCO A-B: 1960 only, painted blue	150	225	350	6
225 CHESAPEAKE & OHIO ALCO A: 1960 only, painted dark blue	75	125	175	4
226 B & M ALCO A-B: 1960 only, B unit always unpainted blue plastic				
A unit unpainted blue	100.	175	275	5
A unit painted blue	150	225	325	6
227 CANADIAN NATIONAL ALCO A: 1960 only, molded gray body painted green	100	150	200	5
228 CANADIAN NATIONAL ALCO A: 1960 only, uncataloged, body painted green	100	150	200	6
229 MINNEAPOLIS & ST. LOUIS ALCO: 1961-62. Single A	75	100	150	4
A-B combination	125	175	275	5

230 Chesapeake & Ohio Alco A

231 Rock Island Alco A

#	Description	VG	EX	LN	S
230 CHESAPEAKE & OHIO ALCO A: 1961 only, painted dark blue	75	125	175	3
231 ROCK ISLAND ALCO A: 1961-63 painted black with white heat-stamped lettering and a white roofline stripe.				
With broad red stripe	75	125	175	5
Without broad red stripe	225	375	500	7
232 NEW HAVEN ALCO A: 1962, painted overall orange with two narrow black stripes.	75	125	175	5
233 2-4-2 STEAM: 1961-62, with 233W tender .	50	75	125	4
235 2-4-2 STEAM: 1961, supplied with either the 1050T or 1130T tender	150	250	350	7
236 2-4-2 STEAM: 1961-62, supplied with either the 1050T or 1130T tender	20	35	50	2
237 2-4-2 STEAM: 1963-66, Thick or thin running boards, 1061T, 1062T, Slopeback 242T or 1060T tender small streamlined. . . .	30	50	85	2
234W Whistle Tender, 1965-66	60	100	175	3
238 2-4-2 STEAM: 1963-64, furnished with the 234W whistle tender. Thick or thin running boards.	100	150	250	5

240 2-4-2 Steam

241 2-4-2 Steam

244 2-4-2 Steam

246 2-4-2 Steam

#	Description	VG	EX	LN	S
239 2-4-2 STEAM: 1965-66, came with either 242T or 234W tender, add $50 premium for 234W.					
Cab number heat-stamped		30	45	70	3
Cab number rubber-stamped		40	75	100	3
240 2-4-2 STEAM: 1964, uncataloged, came with 242T tender		150	225	375	7
241 2-4-2 STEAM: 1965-66, uncataloged, with 234W tender. Painted white stripe		100	175	275	5
Rubber-stamped white stripe		90	150	240	5
242 2-4-2 STEAM: 1962-66, came with 242T, 1060T, 1061T or 1062T tender		10	20	40	1
243 2-4-2 STEAM: 1960 only, came with the 243W tender		70	100	200	4
244 2-4-2 STEAM: 1960-61, came with either 244T or 1130T tender		25	35	50	2
245 2-4-2 STEAM: 1959, uncataloged, came with 1130T tender		40	70	90	3
246 2-4-2 STEAM: 1959-61, came with either the 1130T or the 244T tender		20	30	40	2

247 2-4-2 Steam

400 Baltimore & Ohio RDC-1

520 Lionel Lines 1-B-0 Electric

#	Description	VG	EX	LN	S
247 2-4-2 STEAM: 1959 only, with 247T tender, with matching blue stripe	45	65	90	3
248 2-4-2 STEAM: 1958, uncataloged, with 1130T.	60	70	85	4
249 2-4-2 STEAM: 1958 only, with 250T tender with matching red stripe	30	45	60	3
250 2-4-2 STEAM: 1957 only, with 250T tender with matching red stripe	30	40	50	3
251 2-4-2 STEAM: 1966 only, with 1062T tender.	150	200	350	7
400 BALTIMORE AND OHIO RDC-1: 1956-1958.	150	225	300	3
404 BALTIMORE AND OHIO RDC-4: 1957-58	200	300	400	4
520 LIONEL LINES 1-B-0 ELECTRIC: 1956-57. · Unpainted red plastic body				
Black plastic pantograph.	75	120	175	3
Copper-colored plastic pantograph	100	130	200	4

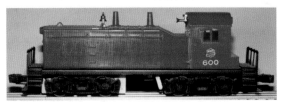

600 M K T NW-2

601 Seaboard NW-2

602 Seaboard NW-2

#	Description	VG	EX	LN	S
600 M K T NW-2: 1955 unpainted red plastic body. Gray frame, yellow platform railings, blued steel steps		375	550	800	6
	Gray frame, blued steel railings and steps	275	425	650	5
	Black frame, blued steel railings and steps	125	175	250	4
	Blued steel frame, blued steel railings and steps	115	160	225	3
601 SEABOARD NW-2: 1956, painted black and red		115	150	225	3
602 SEABOARD NW-2: 1957-58 painted black and red		125	175	250	3
610 ERIE NW-2: 1955-only body painted black, yellow heat-stamped number.					
	Yellow frame and platform railings, blued steel steps	425	650	1100	7
	Black frame, blued steel railings and steps	125	175	250	4
	Blued steel frame, blued steel railings and steps	100	150	225	3
611 JERSEY CENTRAL NW-2: 1957-58, Blue and orange body Unpainted deep blue body		150	225	350	3
	Unpainted light blue body	150	225	350	3
	Painted blue body	400	600	900	6
613 UNION PACIFIC NW-2: 1958 only, yellow and gray		250	400	600	6

614 Alaska Railroad NW-2

616 Santa Fe NW-2

622 A.T. & S.F. NW-2

#	Description	VG	EX	LN	S
614 ALASKA RAILROAD NW-2: 1959-60.					
"BUILT BY / LIONEL" outlined in yellow. .	325	475	750	7
"BUILT BY / LIONEL" unpainted.	150	225	300	4
616 SANTA FE NW-2: 1961-62, painted black with white safety stripes. Open but unused E-unit and bell slots.	125	175	250	4
Plugged E-unit slot and open bell slot.	200	325	450	6
Both E-unit and bell slots plugged	200	325	450	6
617 SANTA FE NW-2: 1963, painted black with white safety stripes. Came with black ornamental bell, silver ornamental horn, head and marker light lenses, and radio antenna . .	150	250	375	6
621 JERSEY CENTRAL NW-2: 1956-57, unpainted blue plastic body	100	150	200	3
622 A.T. & S.F. NW-2: 1949-50, black, die-cast frame. With "622" stamped on the nose of the locomotive	200	325	500	6
Without "622" stamped on the nose of the locomotive.	150	200	350	3
623 A.T. & S.F. NW-2: 1952-54, black, die-cast frame.					
Hood-side handrail retained by 10 stanchions	125	175	250	4
Hood-side handrail retained by three stanchions	100	150	225	3

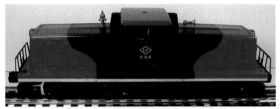

625 Lehigh Valley Center Cab

626 Baltimore & Ohio Center Cab

628 Northern Pacific Center Cab

#	Description	VG	EX	LN	S
624 CHESAPEAKE & OHIO NW-2: 1952-54, medium blue, die-cast frame.					
Hood-side handrail retained by 10 stanchions	150	250	400	5
Hood-side handrail retained by three stanchions	150	225	375	4
Painted light blue........................	300	450	700	7
625 LEHIGH VALLEY CENTER CAB: 1957-58, unpainted red body	125	175	225	4
626 BALTIMORE AND OHIO CENTER CAB: 1957 only, unpainted blue body	250	400	625	6
627 LEHIGH VALLEY CENTER CAB: 1956-57 unpainted red plastic body	75	115	150	2
628 NORTHERN PACIFIC CENTER CAB: 1956-57, unpainted black body	100	150	225	4
629 BURLINGTON CENTER CAB: 1956, silver painted body	250	450	800	7
633 SANTA FE NW-2: 1962, painted blue body with yellow safety stripes	125	200	300	5
634 SANTA FE NW-2: 1963, 1965-66, painted blue body.					
Yellow safety stripes, 1963	125	175	250	4
No stripes, 1965-66	75	125	200	3

637 2-6-4 Steam

646 4-6-4 Steam

665 4-6-4 Steam

671 6-8-6 Steam

#	Description	VG	EX	LN	S
635 UNION PACIFIC NW-2: 1965 only, painted yellow body	75	125	200	5
637 2-6-4 STEAM: 1959-61, with 2046W or 736W tenders. Number rubber-stamped	75	125	200	4
Number heat-stamped	120	175	300	5
638-2361 STOKELY-VAN CAMP'S BOXCAR: 1962-64, uncataloged	25	40	60	5
645 UNION PACIFIC NW-2: 1969, unpainted yellow plastic body	75	125	200	4
646 4-6-4 STEAM: 1954-58, came with 2046W tenders, silver or white cab lettering.	175	250	350	4
665 4-6-4 STEAM: 1954-56, 1966, with 6026W, 2046W or 736W tender. Rubber or heat-stamped numbers on loco	165	250	300	3
671 6-8-6 STEAM: 1946-49, 1946 locos have bulb-type smoke units, heater units used thereafter. Came with 671W or 2671W tenders, $50-75 premium for latter. "6200" stamped in white on boiler front	175	225	325	4
"6200" decal	135	175	275	3
With 2671W tender with backup lights	325	475	600	7

671 R 6-8-6 Steam

675 2-6-2 Steam

681 6-8-6 Steam

682 6-8-6 Steam

# Description	VG	EX	LN	S
671R 6-8-6 STEAM: 1946-49 "Electronic Control."				
Bulb-type smoke unit	250	350	475	7
Heater-type smoke unit.	225	325	425	6
671 RR 6-8-6 STEAM: 1952-only, came with 2046W-50 tender. Without "RR" suffix				
stamped on cab	185	275	350	5
With "RR" suffix stamped on cab	225	350	450	6
675 2-6-2 STEAM: 1947-49, with 2466WX or 6466WX tender.				
White "675" stamped on boiler front.	125	175	250	5
Red keystone decal on boiler front	95	145	225	2
675 2-6-4 STEAM: 1952 only, with 2046W tender.	95	145	225	3
681 6-8-6 STEAM: 1950-51, 1953. 1950-51, 2671W, loco number stamped in silver	175	275	375	3
1953 2046W-50, tender loco number stamped in white	165	250	350	4
682 6-8-6 STEAM: 1954-55, came with a 2046W-50 tender	275	425	600	5
685 4-6-4 STEAM: 1953-only, came with 6026W tender. Rubber numbers.	250	350	500	6
Heat-stamped numbers	200	300	400	5

726 2-8-4 Steam

736 2-8-4 Steam

746 4-8-4 Steam

773 4-6-4 Steam

# Description	VG	EX	LN	S
726 2-8-4 STEAM: 1946-49, with 2426W tender.				
1946, bulb-type smoke units	300	475	600	5
1947-49 heater-type smoke unit	225	350	475	4
726 RR 2-8-4 STEAM: 1952-only, came with 2046W tender.				
Without "RR" suffix stamped on cab	225	375	475	4
With "RR" suffix stamped on cab	300	425	600	5
736 2-8-4 STEAM: 1950-51, 1953-68.				
With 2671WX.	300	425	575	4
With 2046W or 736W tender.	200	300	400	4
746 4-8-4 STEAM: 1957-60.				
Short-striped 746W without number stamping	650	850	1200	5
Long-striped tender stamped 746W	700	900	1500	6
773 4-6-4 STEAM: 1950 with 2426W tender . . .	950	1200	1900	6
1964 with Pennsy 736W tender.	600	850	1200	4
1964-66 with 773W NYC tender	750	900	1500	4
1001 2-4-2 STEAM: 1948 only, all with 1001T tender. Plastic boiler, silver numbers	90	125	175	6
Plastic boiler, white numbers	25	40	60	2
Die-cast boiler	225	325	450	7
1002 LIONEL GONDOLA: 1948-52. Black, or blue	7	10	15	1
Red, silver or yellow	225	375	500	5

X1004 Baby Ruth Boxcar

1005 Sunoco Tank Car

1060 2-4-2 Steam

#	Description	VG	EX	LN	S
X1004 BABY RUTH BOXCAR: 1948-52, outline or solid lettering	6	10	14	1
1005 SUNOCO TANK CAR: 1948-50, gray tank.				
Medium blue lettering	5	7	12	1
Dark blue lettering	5	7	12	2
1007 LIONEL LINES CABOOSE: 1948-52.				
Red body	2	4	6	2
Tuscan body.	75	200	300	7
1050 0-4-0 STEAM: 1959-only, came with a 1050T slope-back tender	150	200	350	6
1055 TEXAS SPECIAL ALCO A: 1959-60, painted red with white lettering	40	60	90	2
1060 2-4-2 STEAM: 1960-62, came with 1050T or 1060T tender. Long or short rainshield over loco headlight	10	25	50	1
1061 0-4-0 or 2-4-2 STEAM: 1963-64, 1969 used 1061T, 1062T, 1060T or 242T tenders.				
White heat stamped cab numbers	10	25	45	1
No cab numbers	110	200	250	5
Cab numbers on paper label	150	225	300	7

1062 0-4-0 Steam

1065 Union Pacific Alco A

1130 2-4-2 Steam

1615 0-4-0 Steam

#	Description	VG	EX	LN	S
1062 0-4-0 or 2-4-2 STEAM: 1963-64 used 1061T, 1062T, 1060T or 242T tenders.					
With Lionel Lines or undecorated tender . . .	10	20	35	1
With Southern Pacific tender	95	125	175	6
1065 UNION PACIFIC ALCO A: 1961-only, body painted yellow	45	65	100	2
1066 UNION PACIFIC ALCO A: 1964, uncataloged unpainted yellow body	45	65	100	2
1101 2-4-2 STEAM: 1948-only, with 1001T tender	15	35	55	3
1110 2-4-2 STEAM: 1949, 1951-52 with 1001T tender. Baldwin disc drive wheels.	25	40	60	3
Spoked drive wheels.	10	20	35	1
1120 2-4-2 STEAM: 1950-only, with 1001T tender	15	30	50	2
1130 2-4-2 STEAM: 1953-54, with 6066T or 1130T tender. Die-cast boiler	225	350	450	7
Plastic boiler, silver rubber-stamped numbers	10	25	40	3
Plastic boiler, white heat-stamped numbers . .	30	70	100	5
1615 0-4-0 STEAM: 1955-57, with 1615T tender.	125	175	275	3

1625 0-4-0 Steam

1862 4-4-0 Steam

1866 Western & Atlantic Mail-Baggage

#	Description	VG	EX	LN	S
1625 0-4-0 STEAM: 1958-only, with 1625T tender.	175	275	400	6
1654 2-4-2 STEAM: 1946-47.				
With 1654T tender.	30	50	70	3
With 1654W tender	35	60	95	3
1655 2-4-2 STEAM: 1948-49, with 6654W tender.	40	70	95	3
1656 0-4-0 STEAM: 1948-49, with 6403B tender.				
Separate Bakelite coal pile	225	350	475	6
Integral die-cast coal pile	200	300	425	5
1665 0-4-0 STEAM: 1946 only, with 2403B tender.				
Heat-stamped tender lettering.	200	325	450	5
Rubber-stamped tender lettering	250	375	500	6
1666 2-6-2 STEAM: 1946-47.				
Number plate beneath cab window	75	100	175	3
Number rubber-stamped beneath cab window	100	150	250	5
1862 4-4-0 STEAM: 1959-62, with 1862T tender.	125	200	300	3
1865 WESTERN & ATLANTIC COACH: 1959-62, body painted yellow with brown roof.	20	30	40	3

1872 4-4-0 Steam

1875 Western & Atlantic Coach

1877 Flatcar

#	Description	VG	EX	LN	S
1866 WESTERN & ATLANTIC MAIL-BAGGAGE: 1959-62, body painted yellow with brown roof	20	30	40	3
1872 4-4-0 STEAM: 1959-62, with 1872T tender.	150	250	350	4
1875 WESTERN & ATLANTIC COACH: 1959-62, body painted yellow with brown roof.	125	200	275	5
1875W WESTERN & ATLANTIC COACH WITH WHISTLE: 1959-62, body painted yellow with brown roof	60	100	140	3
1876 WESTERN & ATLANTIC MAIL-BAGGAGE: 1959-62, body painted yellow with brown roof	40	65	90	3
1877 FLATCAR: 1959-62, unpainted brown plastic, came with a load of two white, two tan and brown, and two black horses made by Bachmann Bros. (hence the "BB" logo on the horses' bellies), and a 10-section maroon fence.	35	75	110	4
1882 4-4-0 STEAM: 1960-only, came with 1882T tender.	425	550	800	7
1885 WESTERN & ATLANTIC COACH: 1960, painted blue with brown roof.	175	250	350	6

2016 2-6-4 Steam

2018 2-6-4 Steam

2023 Union Pacific Alco A-A

2024 Chesapeake & Ohio Alco A

#	Description	VG	EX	LN	S
1887 FLATCAR: 1960-only, unpainted brown plastic, came with a load of two white, two tan and brown, and two black horses made by Bachmann Bros. (hence the "BB" logo on the horses' bellies), and a ten-section fence	140	200	275	6
2016 2-6-4 STEAM: 1955-56, with 6026W tender.				
Number heat-stamped	75	100	175	3
Number rubber-stamped	150	250	350	5
2018 2-6-4 STEAM: 1956-59.				
With 6026T or 1130T tender	50	65	100	2
With 6026W tender	65	100	150	2
2020 6-8-6 STEAM: 1946-49, 1946 locos have bulb-type smoke units, heater units used thereafter. "6200" stamped in white on some boiler fronts, decalled on most, came with 2020W or 6020W tender. "6200" stamped in white on boiler front	175	225	350	4
"6200" decal	150	225	285	3
With heater-type smoke unit	165	225	325	3
2023 UNION PACIFIC ALCO A-A: 1950-51.				
Yellow with gray roof and nose	2000	2800	4000	8
Yellow with gray roof	175	300	450	4
Silver with gray roof	175	300	450	4
2024 CHESAPEAKE & OHIO ALCO A: 1969 only, unpainted dark blue body	40	60	90	3

2018 2-6-4 Steam

2028 Pennsylvania GP-7

2029 2-6-4 Steam

2031 Rock Island Alco A-A

#	Description	VG	EX	LN	S
2025 2-6-2 STEAM: 1947-49, came with 2466WX or 6466WX tender.					
	White "2025" stamped on boiler front......	85	125	200	5
	Red keystone decal on boiler front	70	100	175	2
2025 2-6-4 STEAM: 1952 only, with 6466W					
	tender..................................	85	125	200	3
2026 2-6-2 STEAM: 1948-49, with 6466WX tender.					
	Baldwin disc........................	75	100	150	4
	Spoke wheels	50	75	100	2
2026 2-6-4 STEAM: 1951-53, with 6066T, 6466T or 6466W tender. Reduce listed values one third for non-whistling tenders.					
	Number rubber-stamped in silver	65	95	150	2
	Number heat-stamped in white...........	90	125	185	3
2028 PENNSYLVANIA GP-7: 1955.					
	Gold rubber-stamped lettering, gold frame..	250	425	650	6
	Yellow rubber-stamped lettering, gold frame.	225	350	500	5
	Tan frame	350	600	900	8
2029 2-6-4 STEAM: 1964-69. Reduce listed values one third for non-whistling tenders. With 1060T, 234T or 234W "Lionel Lines"					
	tender.................................	55	75	125	4
	With 234W "Pennsylvania" tender	250	275	325	7
	"Made in Japan."	65	100	150	5

2032 Erie Alco A-A

2037 2-6-4 Steam

2037-500 2-6-4 Steam

2041 Rock Island Alco A-A

# Description	VG	EX	LN	S
2031 ROCK ISLAND ALCO A-A: 1952-54 painted black with broad red stripe	250	375	550	6
2032 ERIE ALCO A-A: 1952-54 painted black with narrow yellow striping	150	225	350	4
2033 UNION PACIFIC ALCO A-A: 1952-54 painted silver with silver roof.............	175	275	450	3
2034 2-4-2 STEAM: 1952-only, came with a 6066T tender........................	15	35	60	2
2035 2-6-4 STEAM: 1950-51 came with the 6466W tender	85	125	200	3
2036 2-6-4 STEAM: 1950-only, with 6466W tender...............................	100	150	225	2
2037 2-6-4 STEAM: 1953-55, 1957-63, came with 6026W, 233W or 234W whistle tender, or non-whistling 6066T, 6026T or 1130T tender. Reduce the values listed one third for non-whistle tender......................	75	120	175	2
2037-500 2-6-4 STEAM: 1957-58, pink, with 1130T-500 pink tender	500	700	950	6
2041 ROCK ISLAND ALCO A-A: 1969, unpainted black plastic bodies with wide red stripe	75	115	150	3

2056 4-6-4 Steam

2065 4-6-4 Steam

2240 Wabash F-3 A-B

2242 New Haven F-3 A-B

# Description	VG	EX	LN	S
2046 4-6-4 STEAM: 1950-51, 1953, came with 2046W tender.				
Silver numbers with die-cast trailing truck ..	140	200	275	3
White numbers with plastic and sheet-metal trailing truck	140	200	275	3
2055 4-6-4 STEAM: 1953-55, came with 6026W or 2046W tender.......................	140	200	275	3
2056 4-6-4 STEAM: 1952-only, came with 2046W tender.........................	175	250	350	3
2065 4-6-4 STEAM: 1954-56, came with 6026W or 2046W tender......................	175	250	325	4
2240 WABASH F-3 A-B: 1956 only, molded in medium blue painted blue with the roof and upper body painted gray, the white band was silk-screened on. The final segment of the B-unit's white stripe, near "Built by Lionel" is 1/2-inch long.	500	750	1150	4
2242 NEW HAVEN F-3 A-B: 1958-59, heat-stamped white "NH" on the nose door.	750	1250	2000	6
2243 SANTA FE F-3 A-B: 1955-57.				
High-profile molded cab door ladder.	350	500	750	3
Flush molded cab door ladder.	300	450	675	3

2245 The Texas Special F-3 A-B

2321 Lackawanna FM

2329 Virginian EL-C Rectifier

# Description	VG	EX	LN	S
2243 C SANTA FE F-3 B UNIT: 1955-57, not originally sold separately, but often sold individually on the collector market.	150	225	300	3
2245 THE TEXAS SPECIAL F-3 A-B: 1954-55, painted glossy red with white silk-screened lower panels. The red lettering on the sides of the units was actually the red paint that had been masked off. Horizontal motor in 1954. .	400	550	800	5
Vertical motor, B-unit with open portholes . .	450	600	900	5
Late 1955 B-unit with molded closed porthole	750	1000	1500	7
2257 LIONEL-SP CABOOSE: 1947.				
Red or red-orange no stack	3	5	10	2
Red-orange with matching stack	100	225	400	6
Tuscan with matching stack.	300	500	775	8
2321 LACKAWANNA FM: 1954-56. Maroon roof	550	800	1250	6
Gray roof	375	500	750	4
2322 VIRGINIAN FM: 1965-66.				
Unpainted blue plastic with painted-on yellow trim	400	600	800	4
Both blue and yellow painted on	500	750	950	6
2328 BURLINGTON GP-7: 1955-56, painted silver body, red frame.	300	450	750	4
2329 VIRGINIAN EL-C RECTIFIER: 1958-59, blue-painted body with yellow frame.	500	800	1250	5

2331 Virginian FM

2332 Pennsylvania GG1

2338 The Milwaukee Road GP-7

# Description	VG	EX	LN	S
2330 PENNSYLVANIA GG1: 1950, painted green	800	1400	2200	5
2331 VIRGINIAN FM: 1955-58. Molded gray body painted yellow and blue	1000	1350	2100	7
Molded gray body painted black and yellow	850	1200	1750	6
Molded blue body with yellow painted on	600	800	1150	5
2332 PENNSYLVANIA GG1: 1947-49. Green	300	450	750	3
VERY dark, almost black green	600	1000	1800	8
2333 SANTA FE F-3 A-A: 1948-49.				
Clear, unpainted body	3000	5000	7000	8
Silver and red painted body	300	600	1200	4
2334 NEW YORK CENTRAL F-3 A-A: 1948-49.				
Rubber-stamped lettering	350	650	1300	5
Heat-stamped lettering	300	600	1200	4
2337 WABASH GP-7: 1958, unpainted blue plastic body	250	350	525	5
2338 THE MILWAUKEE ROAD GP-7: 1955-56. Translucent orange plastic body with orange stripe on cab	1000	1500	2250	6
Translucent orange plastic body with no cab stripe	175	275	400	4
Opaque orange plastic bodies with no cab stripe	175	275	400	3

2343 Santa Fe F-3 A-A

2344 New York Central F-3 A-A

2346 Boston & Maine GP-9

2347 Chesapeake & Ohio GP-7

# Description	VG	EX	LN	S
2339 WABASH GP-7: 1957, unpainted blue plastic body	200	300	450	5
2340 PENNSYLVANIA GG1: 1955. Painted green	800	1250	2200	5
Painted Tuscan red	1000	1500	2650	6
2341 JERSEY CENTRAL FM: 1956 only, molded blue plastic body. Gloss orange	1500	2350	3500	7
Matte orange paint	1250	2000	2850	6
2343 SANTA FE F-3 A-A: 1950-52, painted red and silver	300	500	1200	3
2343 C SANTA FE F-3 B-UNIT: 1950-55. Screen-type (50-51) or molded louver roof vents	150	250	450	4
2344 NEW YORK CENTRAL F-3 A-A: 1950-52	350	600	1100	3
2344 C NEW YORK CENTRAL F-3 B-UNIT: 1950-55. Screen-type (50-51) or molded louver roof vents	175	300	450	4
2345 WESTERN PACIFIC F-3 A-A: 1952 painted silver and orange	1250	2100	3300	6
2346 BOSTON AND MAINE GP-9: 1965-66, black plastic body painted blue	200	300	425	4

DUMMY

2348 Minneapolis & St. Louis GP-9

2349 Northern Pacific GP-9

2350 New Haven EP-5

# Description	VG	EX	LN	S
2347 CHESAPEAKE & OHIO GP-7: 1965 only, body painted blue with yellow heat-stamped markings	1500	2500	3600	8
2348 MINNEAPOLIS & ST LOUIS GP-9: 1958-59, painted red, and a white stripe painted on the middle of each side, the cab roof was painted blue, and red and white lettering was heat-stamped on	250	350	500	5
2349 NORTHERN PACIFIC GP-9: 1959-60, painted black brilliant gold-painted ends and side stripes	300	450	600	6
2350 NEW HAVEN EP-5: 1956-58.				
Orange "N", a black "H", painted nose	1000	1600	2500	8
Orange "N", a black "H", decal nose	700	1200	1800	7
White "N", orange "H", painted nose	500	750	1100	6
White "N", orange "H", decal nose	300	400	550	3
2351 MILWAUKEE ROAD EP-5: 1957-58, yellow-painted body with a maroon-painted stripe in the middle and a black-painted upper quarter and roof, heat-stamped yellow lettering	350	500	750	6
2352 PENNSYLVANIA EP-5: 1957-58, Tuscan-painted body	350	500	750	5

2355 Western Pacific F-3 A-A

2356 Southern F-3 A-A

2356 C Southern F-3 B-Unit

2358 Great Northern EP-5

# Description	VG	EX	LN	S
2353 SANTA FE F-3 A-A: 1953-55, painted silver and red	350	650	1100	3
2354 NEW YORK CENTRAL F-3 A-A: 1953-55.	300	550	950	4
2355 WESTERN PACIFIC F-3 A-A: 1953, silver and orange paint	1100	1800	3000	7
2356 SOUTHERN F-3 A-A: 1954-56 green-painted body had its lower side panels and nose painted gray with rubber-stamped yellow stripes and lettering	800	1250	2100	5
2356 C SOUTHERN F-3 B-UNIT: 1954-56 decorated to match the 2356 A-A units	275	400	550	6
2357 LIONEL-SP CABOOSE: 1947-48.				
Tuscan body and stack	18	25	30	2
Tile red body no stack	65	125	200	5
Red body and stack	250	450	700	8
2358 GREAT NORTHERN EP-5: 1959-60 "Great Northern" heat-stamped on sides in yellow, end markings, number and "BLT BY LIONEL" were a large decal	700	1100	1800	6
2359 BOSTON AND MAINE GP-9: 1961-62, black plastic body painted blue, cab painted black, white heat-stamped lettering	200	300	450	4

POWER

2363 Illinois Central F-3 A-B

2365 Chesapeake & Ohio GP-7

2368 Baltimore & Ohio F-3 A-B

2373 Canadian Pacific F-3 A-A

# Description	VG	EX	LN	S
2360 PENNSYLVANIA GG1: 1956-58. Green				
with five stripes	800	1400	2400	6
Tuscan with five stripes	900	1500	2500	6
Tuscan with single stripe rubber-stamped ...	750	1300	2200	5
Tuscan with single stripe painted on	750	1100	1750	6
Tuscan with single stripe decal...........	750	1100	1750	6
2363 ILLINOIS CENTRAL F-3 A-B: 1955-56.				
Unpainted orange stripe................	400	800	1500	6
Painted orange stripe	400	800	1500	5
2365 CHESAPEAKE AND OHIO GP-7: 1962-				
63, painted blue with yellow heat-stamped				
markings	200	325	475	4
2367 WABASH F-3 A-B: 1955-only molded				
in royal blue plastic, A unit painted, B-unit				
unpainted. The final segment of white stripe				
on B unit, near the "Built by Lionel" marking				
is 1/8-inch long				
Rubber-stamped B-unit lettering	1200	1900	3100	7
Heat-stamped B-unit lettering	725	1150	1750	5
2368 BALTIMORE AND OHIO F-3 A-B: 1956-				
only. Unpainted blue plastic.............	1600	2400	3500	6
Blue-painted gray plastic body...........	2000	2800	4000	7
2373 CANADIAN PACIFIC F-3 A-A: 1957,				
painted gray and brown with yellow heat-				
stamped stripes and lettering	1200	1800	2900	6

2378 Milwaukee Road F-3 A-B

2379 Rio Grande F-3 A-B

2400 Maplewood Pullman

2404 Santa Fe Vista Done

#	Description	VG	EX	LN	S
2378 MILWAUKEE ROAD F-3 A-B: 1956-only, unpainted gray bodies, painted-on red stripe and yellow heat-stamped delineating stripes. Each unit with or without a thin yellow roofline stripe, matched combinations are preferred.		1500	2400	3300	6
2379 RIO GRANDE F-3 A-B: 1957-58, painted yellow, black horizontal stripes and side lettering were heat-stamped.		1100	1600	2400	5
2383 SANTA FE F-3 A-A: 1958-66, silver and red, or silver and orange-red.		300	450	700	3
2400 MAPLEWOOD PULLMAN: 1948-49, painted green with yellow stripes and window outlines, dark gray roof.		90	140	200	4
2401 HILLSIDE OBSERVATION: 1948-49, matches 2400.		85	125	175	4
2402 CHATHAM PULLMAN: 1948-49, matches 2400.		90	140	200	4
2404 SANTA FE VISTA DONE: 1964-65, no lights or silhouetted window strips		35	70	100	2
2405 SANTA FE PULLMAN: 1964-65, matches 2404.		35	70	100	2

2408 Santa Fe Vista Dome

2411 Flatcar

2414 Santa Fe Pullman

#	Description	VG	EX	LN	S
2406 SANTA FE OBSERVATION: 1964-65, matches 2404		30	60	90	2
2408 SANTA FE VISTA DOME: 1966-only, has lights and silhouetted window strips		40	70	100	2
2409 SANTA FE PULLMAN: 1966-only, matches 2408		40	70	100	2
2410 SANTA FE OBSERVATION: 1966-only, matches 2408		35	60	90	2
2411 FLATCAR: 1946-48. Loaded with steel pipe with groove inside		75	100	140	5
Loaded with 3/8-inch diameter wooden dowels		20	30	42	3
2412 SANTA FE VISTA DOME: 1959-63, blue stripe, illuminated, with silhouetted window strips		30	60	90	3
2414 SANTA FE PULLMAN: 1959-63, matches 2412		30	60	90	3
2416 SANTA FE OBSERVATION: 1959-63, matches 2412		25	55	80	3
2419 D. L. & W WRECKING CAR: 1946-47		25	35	50	3

REPRO LOAD (handwritten)

2420 D. L. & W Wrecking Car

2421 Maplewood Pullman
2422 Chatham Pullman
2423 Hillside Observation

# Description	VG	EX	LN	S
2420 D. L. & W WRECKING CAR: 1946-47, dark gray cab, die-cast frame.				
Dark gray heat-stamped lettering..........	60	100	150	4
Light gray frame, rubber-stamped sans-serif lettering................................	150	200	300	7
Light gray frame, heat-stamped serif lettering................................	75	125	175	5
Dark gray frame, rubber-stamped sans-serif lettering................................	125	175	275	6
2421 MAPLEWOOD PULLMAN:				
1950-51 gray roof......................	60	90	125	3
1952-53 silver roof....................	50	75	100	3
2422 CHATHAM PULLMAN: matches 2421.				
1950-51 gray roof......................	60	90	125	3
1952-53 silver roof....................	50	75	100	3
2423 HILLSIDE OBSERVATION: matches 2421.				
1950-51 gray roof......................	60	80	100	3
1952-53 silver roof....................	50	70	90	3
2429 LIVINGSTON PULLMAN: 1952-53, matches 2421.	90	125	180	4
2430 PULLMAN: 1946-47 sheet-metal with blue body with silver roof....................	20	50	80	3
2431 OBSERVATION: 1946-47, matches 2430 ..	20	50	80	3

2432 Clifton Vista Dome

2435 Elizabeth Pullman

2440 Pullman

#	Description	VG	EX	LN	S
2432 CLIFTON VISTA DOME: 1954-58, silver, illuminated, with silhouetted window strips and red lettering.	25	50	75	2
2434 NEWARK PULLMAN: 1954-58, matches 2432.	25	50	75	2
2435 ELIZABETH PULLMAN: 1954-58, matches 2432.	40	75	125	4
2436 SUMMIT OBSERVATION: 1954-56, matches 2432.	35	60	100	2
2436 MOOSEHEART OBSERVATION: 1957-58, matches 2432.	35	60	100	2
2440 PULLMAN: 1946-47, two-tone green sheet metal silver rubber-stamped or white heat-stamped lettering..	25	50	75	3
2441 OBSERVATION: 1946-47, two-tone green sheet metal silver rubber-stamped or white heat-stamped lettering.	25	50	75	3
2442 PULLMAN: 1946-48, brown sheet-metal, silver rubber-stamped or white heat-stamped lettering..	25	50	75	3

2446 Summit Pullman

X2454 Baby Ruth Boxcar

X2454 Pennsylvania

#	Description	VG	EX	LN	S
2442 CLIFTON VISTA DOME: 1956 red stripe illuminated with silhouetted window strips. .	75	125	175	4
2443 OBSERVATION: 1946-48, brown sheet-metal, silver rubber-stamped or white heat-stamped lettering..	25	45-55	70-90	3
2444 NEWARK PULLMAN: 1956 matches 2442.	75	125	175	4
2445 ELIZABETH PULLMAN: 1956 matches 2442.	100	175	225	5
2446 SUMMIT PULLMAN: 1956 matches 2442.	75	125	175	4
2452 PENNSYLVANIA GONDOLA: 1945-47	12	20	40	2
2452X PENNSYLVANIA GONDOLA: 1946-47	10	15	20	2
X2454 BABY RUTH BOXCAR: 1946-47	15	25	35	3
X2454 PENNSYLVANIA: 1946-only.				
Orange doors.	125	175	250	7
Brown doors.	80	150	225	6
2456 LEHIGH VALLEY HOPPER: 1948-only, black painted body..	15	25	35	4

2460 Bucyrus Erie Crane, gray cab

2460 Bucyrus Erie Crane, black cab

2465 Sunoco Tanker with offset decal

#	Description	VG	EX	LN	S
2457 PENNSYLVANIA CABOOSE: 1945-47, "477618" on side, red or black window frames. Has illumination and glazed windows.					
Brown body.	60	100	150	5
Red body.	20	30	40	3
X2458 PENNSYLVANIA BOXCAR: 1946-48, brown 9 1/4" double-door automobile car.	20	45	65	3
2460 BUCYRUS ERIE CRANE: 1946-50.					
Gray cab.	125	200	275	5
Black cab.	60	80	100	3
2461 TRANSFORMER CAR: 1947-48.					
Red transformer load.	60	100	150	5
Black transformer load.	45	75	100	4
2465 SUNOCO TANKER: 1946-48.					
"SUNOCO" logo decal centered.	100	150	250	6
"SUNOCO" logo decal offset.	5	8	12	3
2472 PENNSYLVANIA CABOOSE: 1946-47, numbered "477618" on sides, red, no illumination or window glazing.	15	25	35	3
2481 PLAINFIELD PULLMAN: 1950, yellow, red markings, gray roof.	150	225	375	5

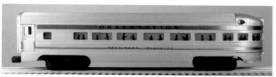

2521 Observation/President McKinley

2523 Pullman/ President Garfield

2530 Lionel Lines / Railway Express Agency

2531 Lionel Lines / Silver Dawn Observation

#	Description	VG	EX	LN	S
2482 WESTFIELD PULLMAN: 1950, matches 2481.		150	225	375	5
2483 LIVINGSTON OBSERVATION: 1950, matches 2481.		125	200	325	5
2521 OBSERVATION / PRESIDENT McKINLEY: 1962-66, extruded aluminum...		75	110	150	3
2522 VISTA DOME / PRESIDENT HARRISON: 1962-66, matches 2521.		75	110	150	3
2523 PULLMAN / PRESIDENT GARFIELD: 1962-66, matches 2521.		75	110	150	3
2530 LIONEL LINES / RAILWAY EXPRESS AGENCY: 1954-60, extruded aluminum baggage car.					
Large doors.		250	400	550	6
Small doors.		75	125	175	4
2531 LIONEL LINES / SILVER DAWN OBSERVATION: 1952-60, extruded aluminum.					
With fluted channels above and below the windows.		60	100	125	3
With flat channels above and below the windows.		125	160	200	6

2532 Lionel Lines/ Silver Range Dome

2533 Lionel Lines / Silver Cloud Pullman

2534 Lionel Lines / Silver Bluff Pullman

2541 Pennsylvania / Alexander Hamilton Observation

#	Description	VG	EX	LN	S
2532 LIONEL LINES / SILVER RANGE DOME: 1952-60, matches 2531. With fluted channels above and below the windows............		60	100	125	3
With flat channels above and below the windows.		125	160	200	6
2533 LIONEL LINES / SILVER CLOUD PULLMAN: 1952-60, matches 2531. With fluted channels above and below the windows.		60	100	125	3
With flat channels above and below the windows.		125	160	200	6
2534 LIONEL LINES / SILVER BLUFF PULLMAN: 1952-60, matches 2531. With fluted channels above and below the windows.		60	100	125	3
With flat channels above and below the windows.		125	160	200	6
2541 PENNSYLVANIA / ALEXANDER HAMILTON OBSERVATION: 1955-56, extruded aluminum.		125	200	275	5
2542 PENNSYLVANIA / BETSY ROSS DOME: 1955-56, matches 2541..................		125	200	275	5
2543 PENNSYLVANIA / WILLIAM PENN PULLMAN: 1955-56, matches 2541........		125	200	275	5
2544 PENNSYLVANIA / MOLLY PITCHER PULLMAN: 1955-56, matches 2541........		125	200	275	5

2551 Canadian Pacific / Banff Park Observation

2552 Canadian Pacific / Skyline 500 Dome

2555 Sunoco Tanker

2560 Lionel Lines Crane

#	Description	VG	EX	LN	S
2550 BALTIMORE AND OHIO RDC-4: 1957-58		350	550	700	6
2551 CANADIAN PACIFIC / BANFF PARK OBSERVATION: 1957 extruded aluminum. .		150	225	325	5
2552 CANADIAN PACIFIC / SKYLINE 500 DOME: 1957, matches 2551.		150	250	325	5
2553 CANADIAN PACIFIC I BLAIR MANOR PULLMAN: 1957, matches 2551		225	350	500	6
2554 CANADIAN PACIFIC / CRAIG MANOR: PULLMAN: 1957, matches 2551		225	350	500	6
2555 SUNOCO TANKER: 1946-48. With "GAS" and "OILS" in SUNOCO logo, "2555" on side.		35	45	60	4
Without "GAS" and "OILS" in SUNOCO logo, "2555" on side		35	45	60	4
With "GAS" and "OILS" in SUNOCO logo, "2555" on bottom.		25	40	55	3
Without "GAS" and "OILS" in SUNOCO logo, "2555" on bottom.		25	40	55	3
2559 BALTIMORE AND OHIO RDC-9: 1957-58 non-powered.		200	300	400	5
2560 LIONEL LINES CRANE: 1946-47 similar to prewar 2660 crane, green, brown or black two-piece boom.		45	65	110	4

2561 Santa Fe / Vista Valley Pullman

2563 Santa Fe / Indian Falls Pullman

2625 Irvington Pullman

2627 Madison Pullman

# Description	VG	EX	LN	S
2561 SANTA FE / VISTA VALLEY PULLMAN: 1959-61, extruded aluminum.	175	225	325	5
2562 SANTA FE / REGAL PASS DOME: 1959-61, matches 2561.	200	250	375	5
2563 SANTA FE / INDIAN FALLS PULLMAN: 1959-61, matches 2561.	200	250	375	5
2625 IRVINGTON PULLMAN: 1946-50.				
Plain windows.	125	225	350	3
Silhouetted windows. (1950 only).	150	275	400	4
2625 MADISON PULLMAN: 1947, plain windows.	175	300	425	4
2625 MANHATTAN PULLMAN: 1947, plain windows.	175	300	425	4
2627 MADISON PULLMAN: 1948-50.				
Plain windows.	125	225	350	3
Silhouetted windows (1950 only).	150	275	400	4
2628 MANHATTAN PULLMAN: 1948-50.				
Plain windows.	125	225	350	3
Silhouetted windows (1950 only).	150	275	400	4
2755 SUNOCO TANKER: 1945-only, silver.	70	100	185	5

2855 Sunoco Tanker

3309 Turbo Missile Launching Car

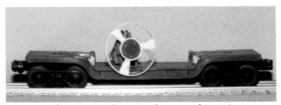

3349 -100 Turbo Missile Launching Car

# Description	VG	EX	LN	S
X2758 PENNSYLVANIA BOXCAR: 1945-46 brown 9 1/4-inch double-door automobile car.	25	50	75	4
2855 SUNOCO TANKER: 1946-47.				
Black, "GAS" and "OILS" in SUNOCO logo	145	225	350	6
Black without "GAS" and "OILS" in SUNOCO logo	145	225	350	6
Gray, without "GAS" and "OILS" in SUNOCO logo	100	175	225	5
3309 TURBO MISSILE LAUNCHING CAR: 1962-64, non-operating couplers.				
Light red.	20	35	55	3
Cherry red.	45	70	100	5
3330 FLATCAR WITH OPERATING SUBMARINE KIT: 1960-62, submarines lettered 3830, those lettered 3330 are forgeries.	100	150	200	5
3349 TURBO MISSILE FIRING CAR: 1962-65, unpainted red plastic, two operating couplers.	30	50	65	4
3349 -100 TURBO MISSILE LAUNCHING CAR: 1963-64, one operating coupler. Red.	20	35	55	3
Olive drab.	200	350	500	7

3356 Santa Fe Horse Car

3357 Hydraulic Platform Maintenance Car

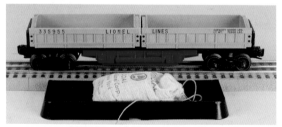

3359 Lionel Lines Dump Car

#	Description	VG	EX	LN	S
3356 SANTA FE HORSE CAR WITH CORRAL: Reduce value by 50 percent if corral is missing.					
	1956-60, bar-end metal	100	140	180	4
	1964-66, AAR-plastic trucks.	124	175	250	5
3357 HYDRAULIC PLATFORM MAINTENANCE CAR: 1962-64, with overhead "bridge," trip and police and hobo figures.	35	65	100	4
3359 LIONEL LINES DUMP CAR: 1955-58. . . .	40	60	80	3
3360 BURRO CRANE: 1956-57, with actuator, yellow. Painted..	425	650	850	6
	Unpainted.	175	275	400	4
3361 LOG DUMP CAR: 1955-59, serif or sans-serif lettering, "336155" either to right or left of "LIONEL LINES".	30	42	55	4
3362 HELIUM TANK UNLOADING CAR: 1961-63, unpainted dark green plastic, white rubber-stamped "LIONEL LINES 3362," three "helium tanks" AAR trucks with operating couplers.	15	20	45	3
3362 /3364 OPERATING UNLOADING CAR: 1969, unpainted dark green plastic, no markings, two "helium tanks," non-operating couplers.	15	35	75	6

3366 Circus Car

3370 Wells Fargo Sheriff And Outlaw

3376 Bronx Zoo

#	Description	VG	EX	LN	S
3364 OPERATING LOG UNLOADING CAR: 1965-66, 1968, Identical to the 3362, and rubber-stamped "3362", came 3 5/8-inch x 6-inch wooden dowels stained brown......		15	30	70	5
3366 CIRCUS CAR: 1959-61 unpainted white body and doors, red-painted roofwalk. Reduce value 50 percent if matching corral and nine white horses are missing.		150	250	350	6
3370 WELLS FARGO SHERIFF AND OUTLAW: 1961-64. Action simulates gunfight.		25	50	75	5
3376 BRONX ZOO: 1960-66, 1969, blue car body. Giraffe "ducks" to avoid obstacle. Includes telltale and operating plate assembly. White or lettering................................		40	65	90	3
Yellow (1969) lettering.		175	300	450	8
3376-160 BRONX ZOO: Green body with yellow lettering.		85	110	150	5
3386 BRONX ZOO: 1960-only, blue with white markings, arch-bar trucks and non-operating couplers..............................		60	80	115	4
3409 OPERATING HELICOPTER LAUNCHING CAR: 1960-62, came with an operating single rotor helicopter with a gray body heat-stamped "NAVY"..............................		100	150	225	6

3410 Helicopter Launching Car

3413 Mercury Capsule Launching Car

3419 Operating Helicopter Launching Car

# Description	VG	EX	LN	S
3410 HELICOPTER LAUNCHING CAR: 1961-63, and carried a gray-bodied single rotor helicopter with heat-stamped "NAVY" with separate pale yellow tail rotor or solid yellow helicopter with integral tail..............	65	100	150	5
3413 MERCURY CAPSULE LAUNCHING CAR: 1962-64, unpainted red plastic chassis with gray plastic superstructure. Came with parachute-equipped rocket..............	100	160	225	6
3413 -150 MERCURY CAPSULE LAUNCHING CAR: 1963, equipped with one operating and one non-operating coupler...............	100	160	225	6
3419 OPERATING HELICOPTER LAUNCHING CAR: 1959-65, its body was made of blue plastic, which ranged from medium blue to a dark, almost purple shade. In 1959 the launch spindle was 2" in diameter, in subsequent years a 1 3/8-inch spindle was used. Black or plated operating mechanism. Single- or two-blade gray "Navy" helicopter.	60	90	150	3
All-yellow helicopter.	80	120	180	3
3424 WABASH BOXCAR WITH BRAKEMAN: 1956-58, with two contractor/pole-support assemblies and two telltale poles. The brakeman figures came in two colors, blue and white, and the car bodies came molded in both medium and dark blue, but there is no difference in value associated with either variation............................	50	75	125	4

3434 Operating Poultry Dispatch

3435 Traveling Aquarium

3444 Erie Operating Gondola

#	Description	VG	EX	LN	S
3428 UNITED STATES MAIL OPERATING BOXCAR: 1959-60, red, white and blue boxcar. Rubber figure of a blue or gray mailman ejects rubber "bag" of mail.		50	85	125	4
3429 U.S.M.C. OPERATING HELICOPTER LAUNCHING CAR: 1960, painted olive drab and white heat-stamped "BUILT BY/ LIONEL U. S. M. C. 3429". Came with single rotor operating helicopter with a gray body heat-stamped "USMC" on the tail boom. . . .		350	425	650	7
3434 OPERATING POULTRY DISPATCH: Man "sweeps" illuminated car with color chicken silhouettes. 1959-60, bar-end metal trucks. . .		75	110	175	5
1964-66, AAR plastic trucks.		65	100	150	4
3435 TRAVELING AQUARIUM: 1959-62, "fish," printed on film, "swim" in illuminated tank. Gold circle around "L" logo and gold "TANK No. 1" and "TANK No. 2" markings.		650	1100	1750	8
Gold "TANK No. 1" and "TANK No. 2" markings, no circle.		550	875	1350	7
Gold markings without "TANK No. 1" and "TANK No. 2" or circle.		200	275	425	6
Yellow markings.		125	200	275	5
3444 ERIE OPERATING GONDOLA: 1957-1959.		50	75	110	3
3451 OPERATING LUMBER CAR: 1946-48, with five unstained 7/16 x 4 5/8-inch wooden dowels.		30	40	60	5

3454 Automatic Merchandise Boxcar

3456 N & W Hopper

3461 Operating Lumber Car, green frame

# Description	VG	EX	LN	S
3454 AUTOMATIC MERCHANDISE BOXCAR:				
1946-47, painted silver. Blue lettering......	80	110	160	4
Red lettering.........................	600	1000	1600	7
3456 N & W HOPPER: 1950-55, operating doors.	25	45	65	3
3459 LIONEL LINES DUMP CAR: 1946-48.				
Aluminum colored dump bin............	150	225	375	6
Green dump bin......................	40	80	110	4
Black dump bin......................	30	50	80	3
3460 FLATCAR WITH TRAILERS: 1955-1957, unpainted green plastic trailers with removable roofs, die-cast landing gear, and metal side signs reading "LIONEL TRAINS"........	40	70	100	4
3461 OPERATING LUMBER CAR: 1949-55.				
Black frame........................	25	35	50	3
Green frame.	30	45	60	4
3462 AUTOMATIC REFRIGERATED MILK CAR: 1947-48, if platform and milk cans are absent, the values should be reduced by 50 percent.				
Gloss cream........................	75	125	200	7
Matte cream.	35	50	70	5
White painted body.	30	45	60	2
X3464 A.T. & S.F. BOXCAR: 1949-52, 9 1/4 inches long. Orange body..............	12	20	30	2
Tan body..........................	275	400	650	7

3469 Lionel Lines Dump Car

Front to rear: 3462 Automatic Refrigerated Milk Car,
3472 Automatic Refrigerated Milk Car, 3482 Automatic Refrigerated Milk Car

# Description	VG	EX	LN	S
X3464 NYC BOXCAR: 1949-52, 9 1/4 inches, tan.	12	20	30	2
3469 LIONEL LINES DUMP CAR: 1949-55, black.	30	40	60	3
3470 AERIAL TARGET LAUNCHING CAR: 1962-64, dark blue flat car.	50	75	100	4
3470 -100 AERIAL TARGET LAUNCHING CAR: 1963, powder blue.	200	325	450	7
3472 AUTOMATIC REFRIGERATED MILK CAR: 1949-53, painted cream or unpainted white with aluminum doors, or unpainted white with plastic doors. If platform and milk cans are absent, the values should be reduced by 50 percent.	30	45	60	2
3474 WESTERN PACIFIC BOXCAR: 1952-53, silver 9 1/4 inches long.	35	55	80	5
3482 AUTOMATIC REFRIGERATED MILK CAR: 1954-55, 9 1/4 inches long unpainted white milk car. Stamped RT3472 or RT3482 to right of door. If platform and milk cans are absent, the values should be reduced by 50 percent.				
Stamped RT3472.	75	100	150	6
Stamped RT3482	40	60	85	5

3494 -150 Missouri Pacific Lines Operating Boxcar

3494-275 State Of Maine Operating Boxcar

3494 -550 Monon Operating Boxcar

#	Description	VG	EX	LN	S
3484 PENNSYLVANIA OPERATING BOXCAR: 1953, 10 5/8 inches long.	30	50	80	3
3484 -25 A T & S F OPERATING BOXCAR: 1954, 1956 Orange 10 5/8 inch long boxcar.				
Black lettering.	900	1100	1800	8
White lettering.	50	80	125	4
3494-1 PACEMAKER OPERATING BOXCAR: 1955 10 5/8 inch long.	75	110	165	4
3494 -150 MISSOURI PACIFIC LINES OPERATING BOXCAR: 1956 10 5/8 inch long.	60	100	160	5
3494-275 STATE OF MAINE OPERATING BOXCAR: 1956-58, 10 5/8 inch long. With "3494275" stamped to the left of the door.	60	80	125	4
Without "3494275" stamped to the left of the door.	100	175	250	6
3494 -550 MONON OPERATING BOXCAR: 1957-58, 10 5/8 inch long.	200	325	500	7
3494-625 SOO LINE OPERATING BOXCAR: 1957-58, 10 5/8 inch long.	200	325	525	7
3509 SATELLITE LAUNCHING CAR: 1961, unpainted dark green, gray and yellow.	40	65	100	5

3520 Lionel Lines Searchlight Car

3530 Electro Mobile Power Generator Car

3535 Operating Security Car With Rotating Searchlight

# Description	VG	EX	LN	S
3510 SATELLITE LAUNCHING CAR: 1962, bright red no number on car.	100	150	225	6
3512 OPERATING FIREMAN AND LADDER CAR: 1959-61. Black extension ladder.	75	125	180	5
Silver extension ladder.	100	160	225	7
3519 OPERATING SATELLITE LAUNCHING CAR: 1961-64, dark green unpainted plastic..	35	55	80	4
3520 LIONEL LINES SEARCHLIGHT CAR: 1952-53, Serif lettering..	75	125	180	6
Sans-serif lettering.	35	55	75	4
3530 ELECTRO MOBILE POWER GENERATOR CAR: 1956-58 through 1958, white stripe stops at ladder, or extends through the molded-in ladder on the right-hand end of the car.	60	100	150	5
3535 OPERATING SECURITY CAR WITH ROTATING SEARCHLIGHT: 1960-61.	75	115	175	4
3540 OPERATING RADAR CAR: 1959-62.	100	175	250	5
3545 OPERATING TV MONITOR CAR: 1961-62.	125	200	275	5
3559 COAL DUMP: 1946-48, black or brown Bakelite mechanism housing..	20	35	50	3

3562 -25 A.T. & S. F. Operating Barrel Car

3562 -50 A.T. & S. F. Operating Barrel Car

3562 -75 A.T. & S. F. Operating Barrel Car

#	Description	VG	EX	LN	S
3562 -1 A.T. & S. F. OPERATING BARREL CAR: 1954. Black with black trough........		110	175	250	4
Black with yellow trough.		110	175	200	4
Gray with red lettering.................		1000	1500	2200	8
3562 -25 A.T. & S. F. OPERATING BARREL CAR: 1954 only.					
Gray painted body marked 356225 on car side. Red heat-stamped markings.............		250	400	625	6
Gray painted body with blue markings......		40	65	85	3
Yellow painted body with black heat-stamped markings...........................		1200	1800	2700	8
3562 -50 A.T. & S. F. OPERATING BARREL CAR: 1955-56, marked 356250 on car side.					
Yellow painted body.		60	95	150	4
Yellow unpainted body.		45	70	85	3
3562 -75 A.T. & S. F. OPERATING BARREL CAR: Orange unpainted body marked 356275.		60	90	150	4
3619 HELICOPTER RECONNAISSANCE CAR: 1962-64. It had an unpainted yellow body, red HO gauge helicopter. Light yellow plastic.		60	100	150	4
Dark yellow plastic...................		100	175	250	6

3650 Lionel Lines Searchlight Extension Car

3656 Lionel Lines Operating Cattle Car

#	Description	VG	EX	LN	S
3620 LIONEL LINES SEARCHLIGHT CAR: 1954-56.					
Searchlight housing made of unpainted gray plastic.	30	40	60	4
Searchlight housing made of unpainted orange plastic.	100	140	200	7
Searchlight housing made of orange plastic painted gray.	125	175	250	7
Searchlight housing made of gray plastic painted gray.	30	40	60	4
3650 LIONEL LINES SEARCHLIGHT EXTENSION CAR: 1956-59, values include die-cast spool handle.					
Light gray frame.	40	60	80	4
Dark gray frame.	80	120	175	6
Olive-gray frame.	125	175	250	7
3656 LIONEL LINES OPERATING CATTLE CAR: 1949-55 Reduce value 50 percent if matching corral and cattle are missing. Heat-stamped black lettering, adhesive "Armour" logo.	150	225	300	7
Heat-stamped white lettering, adhesive "Armour" logo.	60	90	125	6
Heat-stamped white lettering, no "Armour" logo.	50	75	110	4
Heat-stamped black lettering, No "Armour" logo	125	200	275	7

3662 Automatic Refrigerated Milk Car

3665 Minuteman

3666 Minuteman

3672 Corn Products Co.-Bosco

# Description	VG	EX	LN	S
3662 AUTOMATIC REFRIGERATED MILK CAR: 1955-60 and 1964-66. If platform and milk cans are absent, the values should be reduced by 50 percent.				
Painted white, heat-stamped "NEW 4-55"...	50	75	115	5
Unpainted white, heat-stamped "NEW 4-55".....................	45	70	100	4
AAR trucks, unpainted white, heat-stamped "NEW 4-55"..................	50	75	115	5
1964-66 unpainted white, AAR-type trucks, no "NEW 4-55".	45	70	100	4
3665 MINUTEMAN: 1961-64 unpainted white body with red and white rocket with blue rubber nose cone.				
Dark blue, almost purple, roof............	60	90	125	4
Light blue roof......................	150	200	325	7
3666 MINUTEMAN: unpainted white body housing large olive drab cannon with four wooden artillery shells.................	350	550	800	8
3672 CORN PRODUCTS CO.-BOSCO: 1959-60. If platform and milk cans are absent, the values should be reduced by 50 percent.				
Unpainted yellow body.................	225	350	500	6
Painted yellow.	250	375	550	6

3854 Automatic Merchandise Car

3927 Lionel Lines Track Cleaning Car

4452 Pennsylvania Gondola

X4454 Baby Ruth Boxcar

#	Description	VG	EX	LN	S
3820 U.S.M.C. OPERATING SUBMARINE CAR: 1960-62, painted olive drab body carrying factory-assembled gray "U.S. NAVY 3830" submarine. Be aware that in addition to reproduction 3830 submarines, forgeries stamped "U.S.M.C. 3820" also exist.		150	225	350	6
3830 SUBMARINE CAR: 1960-63 unpainted blue carrying submarine lettered "U.S. NAVY 3830".		90	115	150	4
3854 AUTOMATIC MERCHANDISE CAR: 1946-47. Bakelite body painted brown, with 6 plastic "crates" (actually cubes) engraved "BABY RUTH". Cubes came in black, brown and red, with brown being the most common..		375	600	850	8
3927 LIONEL LINES TRACK CLEANING CAR: 1956-60		40	65	90	2
4357 LIONEL-SP CABOOSE: 1948-49, Tuscan-painted plastic body.					
Plastic smokejack painted body color.		85	150	250	5
Die-cast smokejack finished in black.		90	165	265	5
4452 PENNSYLVANIA GONDOLA: 1946-49. . .		75	115	150	4
X4454 BABY RUTH BOXCAR: 1946-49.		100	175	300	6

5459 Lionel Lines Dump Car

X6004 Baby Ruth Boxcar

6014 Airex Boxcar

# Description	VG	EX	LN	S
4457 PENNSYLVANIA CABOOSE: 1946-47, steel-bodied caboose painted red..........	75	150	250	6
5459 LIONEL LINES DUMP CAR: 1946-49.	100	175	275	4
6002 NEW YORK CENTRAL GONDOLA: 1950 only. It was not supplied with a load........	12	20	30	4
X6004 BABY RUTH BOXCAR: 1950 only, unpainted orange	5	7	10	2
6007 LIONEL LINES CABOOSE: 1950 only, unpainted red plastic.	5	10	15	2
6012 LIONEL GONDOLA: 1951-56, unpainted black plastic body.	5	8	15	1
6014 AIREX BOXCAR: 1959 only.	35	50	75	5
X6014 BABY RUTH BOXCAR: 1951-56. These cars had metal trucks.				
Red body with white lettering.............	7	12	16	2
Flat white body and black lettering.	4	8	10	1
Glossy white body with black lettering......	4	8	10	1
6014 BOSCO BOXCAR: 1958 AAR-type trucks.				
Unpainted red body....................	6	9	12	1
Unpainted white body.	30	50	75	6
Unpainted orange body.	6	9	12	1

6014 Chun King Boxcar

6014 WIX Filters Boxcar

6015 Sunoco Tanker

# Description	VG	EX	LN	S
6014 CHUN KING BOXCAR: 1956. . , ...	100	150	250	7
6014 FRISCO BOXCAR: 1957, 1963–69. 1957				
unpainted red body.	4	6	10	1
1957 flat white version.	4	6	10	1
1957 orange.	40	60	80	6
1963 lighter white.	4	6	10	1
With coin slot in the roof.	50	75	125	7
1969 very glossy white.	4	6	10	2
1969 orange.	20	30	45	4
6014 WIX FILTERS BOXCAR: 1959-only.				
Snow white unpainted body.	120	180	280	7
Cream color unpainted body	100	150	250	6
6015 SUNOCO TANKER: 1954-55.				
Painted yellow.	65	100	150	5
Molded medium-yellow.	5	8	10	1
Molded dark-yellow body.	5	8	10	2
6017 LIONEL LINES CABOOSE: 1951-62.				
Unpainted red body, metal trucks.	5	10	15	2
Unpainted Tuscan body supplanted the red previously used. These cars had bar-end trucks and a single magnetic coupler.	4	7	10	1
Semi-gloss Tuscan paint.	50	75	100	6
Distinctly glossy Tuscan red.	75	125	200	7
Painted maroon.	8	12	16	3
Painted tile red.	6	9	12	2
Painted brown.	2	4	6	1

6017 -50 United States Marine Corps Caboose

6017 Boston And Maine Caboose

6017 Boston And Maine Caboose
Dark blue variation

#	Description	VG	EX	LN	S
6017 LIONEL CABOOSE: 1956 only, often mistaken for the common 6017 Lionel Lines.		35	60	90	5
6017 -50 UNITED STATES MARINE CORPS CABOOSE: 1958-only, dark blue.		35	60	90	4
6017 LIONEL LINES CABOOSE: 1958-only, painted light gray..		15	30	45	3
6017 BOSTON AND MAINE CABOOSE: 1959, 1962, and 1965-66.					
Painted medium-blue.		20	35	60	4
Semi-gloss medium-blue bodies.		15	30	50	3
Semi-gloss light blue.		15	30	50	3
Painted dark blue; almost purple.		275	425	650	6
6017 A.T.&S.F. CABOOSE: 1959-60, painted light gray.		20	30	45	4
6017 -200 UNITED STATES NAVY CABOOSE: 1960-only.		50	75	110	5
6017 -235 A. T. & S. F. CABOOSE: 1962 only, painted red.		30	50	75	4
6024 RCA WHIRLPOOL BOXCAR: 1957 only.		35	60	80	5
6024 SHREDDED WHEAT BOXCAR: 1957 only.		12	20	30	3

6025 Gulf Tank Car

6027 Alaska Railroad Caboose

6032 Lionel Gondola

#	Description	VG	EX	LN	S
6025 GULF TANK CAR: 1956-58.					
Unpainted black plastic body with white rubber-stamped lettering..	5	10	15	2
Painted-black body with white rubber-stamped lettering.	5	10	15	3
Unpainted gray body with blue heat-stamped lettering..	5	10	15	3
Orange body with blue lettering.	16	25	40	4
6027 ALASKA RAILROAD CABOOSE: 1949-only, painted dark blue, heat-stamped in yellow.	40	65	95	5
6032 LIONEL GONDOLA: 1952-54, unpainted black plastic..	5	8	15	2
X6034 BABY RUTH BOXCAR: 1953-54 unpainted orange.	7	10	14	1
6035 SUNOCO TANK CAR: 1952-53, unpainted gray body.	3	8	15	1
6037 LIONEL LINES CABOOSE: 1952-54.					
Unpainted Tuscan bodies.	3	5	7	1
Unpainted red bodies with white heat stamped markings.	25	40	65	4

6044 Airex Boxcar

6045 Lionel Lines Tank Car

6045 Cities Service Tank Car

# Description	VG	EX	LN	S
6042 LIONEL GONDOLA: 1959-64 equipped with archbar or AAR trucks, with or without operating couplers. Black.	5	8	12	2
Blue.	5	8	12	2
Blue, unmarked.	10	15	18	2
6044 AIREX BOXCAR: 1959-61. White and yellow heat-stamped lettering, medium blue..	10	18	25	3
Teal blue body.	55	85	125	6
Very dark blue, approaching purple.	175	275	400	8
6044 -1X McCALL'S-NESTLE'S BOXCAR: Produced in the early 1960s, unpainted blue body was decorated by pasting a miniature McCall's-Nestle's billboard on each side.	700	1000	1800	8
6045 LIONEL LINES TANK CAR: 1959-64. Unpainted gray.	15	30	45	3
Unpainted beige	15	30	45	3
Unpainted orange	20	50	75	4
6045 CITIES SERVICE TANK CAR: 1960-61, green.	20	50	75	4
6047 LIONEL LINES CABOOSE: 1959-62. Unpainted medium red.	3	5	10	2
Unpainted coral-pink	20	40	65	5

6050 Libby's Tomato Juice Boxcar

6050 Lionel Savings Bank Boxcar

6058 Chesapeake And Ohio Caboose

#	Description	VG	EX	LN	S
6050 LIBBY'S TOMATO JUICE BOXCAR: 1963, unpainted white body with red and blue lettering and a red, blue and green tomato juice logo...........................		20	35	60	4
6050 LIONEL SAVINGS BANK BOXCAR: 1961.					
"BUILT BY LIONEL" abbreviated as "BLT".		20	30	45	4
"BUILT BY LIONEL" spelled out........		50	75	100	6
6050 SWIFT BOXCAR: 1962-63.					
Unpainted red with white heat-stamped lettering....................		12	20	30	3
With two holes in the roofwalk, a leftover from 3357......................		30	50	90	6
6057 LIONEL LINES CABOOSE: 1959-62, 1969.					
Painted red.		35	60	90	6
Unpainted red.		6	10	15	2
Coral-pink bodies.		25	45	65	4
6057 -50 LIONEL LINES CABOOSE: 1962,					
unpainted orange.....................		15	25	40	3
6058 CHESAPEAKE AND OHIO CABOOSE:					
1961, painted dark yellow.		20	35	60	5
6059 M & St L CABOOSE: 1961-69.					
Painted red.		15	20	30	5
Unpainted red.....................		4	8	12	3
Unpainted maroon		8	10	16	4

6076 A T S F Hopper

6076 Lehigh Valley Hopper

6076 Lehigh Valley Hopper

# Description	VG	EX	LN	S
6059 -50 M & St L: 1963-64, unpainted red body with white heat-stamped markings.........	12	18	25	5
6062 NEW YORK CENTRAL GONDOLA: 1959-1962, 1969.				
Black, with metal underframe............	25	40	60	5
Unpainted black, no metal underframe......	15	20	28	2
Painted black.	15	20	28	2
6067 CABOOSE: 1961-62. Unlettered, red unpainted plastic.......................	2	4	7	1
Yellow plastic.........................	12	20	35	3
Brown plastic	20	35	50	4
6076 A T S F HOPPER: Unpainted gray, black heat-stamped lettering.	15	30	40	4
6076 LEHIGH VALLEY HOPPER: 1961-65.				
Light red body........................	10	14	18	2
Dark red body.	10	14	18	2
Black body............................	10	14	18	2
Gray body.	10	14	18	2
Pale yellow-painted body..................	400	800	1800	8
6110 2-4-2 STEAM: 1950 only, with a 6001T tender.	25	40	55	2

6112 Lionel Gondola, white

6119 D.L.&W. Work Caboose

6119-25 D. L. & W. Work Caboose

#	Description	VG	EX	LN	S
6111 /6121 FLATCAR: 1955-58.					
	Fire engine red with white lettering.	10	15	20	3
	Bright red with white lettering.	10	15	20	3
	Maroon with white lettering.	30	50	80	7
	Medium lemon yellow with black lettering. . .	10	15	20	3
	Medium lemon yellow with white lettering. . .	200	350	500	8
	Light gray with white lettering.	10	15	20	3
	Glossy dark gunmetal gray with white lettering.	10	15	20	3
	Gray-drab with white lettering.	10	15	20	3
	Dark gray with white lettering.	10	15	20	3
	Battleship gray with white lettering.	10	15	20	3
6112 LIONEL GONDOLA: 1956-58.					
	Black body with white lettering.	5	8	12	1
	Blue body with white lettering.	10	14	18	2
	White body with black lettering.	15	30	50	4
6119 D.L.&W. WORK CABOOSE: 1955-56, unpainted red open tool compartment and unpainted red plastic cab.		12	25	40	3
6119 -25 D.L.&W. WORK CABOOSE: 1956 only, overall orange work caboose.		20	35	55	4
6119 -50 D. L. & W. WORK CABOOSE: 1956 only, all-brown 6119.		25	45	75	5

6119 -75 D.L.&W. Work Caboose

6119 -100 D.L.&W. Work Caboose

6119 -125 Rescue Caboose

#	Description	VG	EX	LN	S
6119 -75 D.L.&W. WORK CABOOSE: 1957. Unpainted gray tool compartment and cab, black heat-stamped sans-serif lettering......		12	25	45	4
Closely spaced, black rubber-stamped serif lettering on its frame.		125	225	350	8
6119 -100 D.L.&W. WORK CABOOSE: 1957-66. Unpainted gray tool compartment and an unpainted red cab.....................		8	15	25	2
Cab painted red......................		60	100	150	6
With builder's plate heat stamped "BUILT BY / LIONEL".........................		75	125	175	6
6119 -125 RESCUE CABOOSE: 1964 only. Cab and tool compartment unpainted olive drab plastic.		100	175	250	6
6120 UNDECORATED CABOOSE: Unpainted yellow tool compartment and cab..........		20	30	40	3
6130 A. T. S. F. CABOOSE: 1961-65, 1969. Red tool compartment and a red cab...........		16	25	40	4
1966 with additional, but unused letterboard.		90	150	225	7

6142 Lionel Gondola

6151 Flatcar With Range Patrol Truck

6162 New York Central Gondola

#	Description	VG	EX	LN	S
6142 LIONEL GONDOLA: 1963-66, 1969.					
	Black body............................	5	8	12	1
	Unlettered green body................	10	12	15	2
	Unlettered bright translucent green body.	30	40	50	4
	Blue body stamped "Lionel" and "6142".....	5	8	10	1
	Green body stamped "Lionel" and "6142". ..	5	8	10	1
	Undecorated olive drab body; listed as 6142-75 in the Lionel Service Manual.	75	110	165	5
6151 FLATCAR WITH RANGE PATROL TRUCK: 1958 only, white cabbed-black bodied truck made by Pyro heat stamped "LIONEL RANCH"............................		65	110	160	5
6162 NEW YORK CENTRAL GONDOLA: 1959-68, commonly with a load of three white canisters.					
	Blue body with "NEW 2-49" markings on car sides..................................	10	12	15	1
	Teal body with "NEW 2-49" markings on car sides.	10	12	15	1
	Blue without "NEW 2-49" markings.	10	12	15	1
	Red, without "NEW 2-49" markings.	85	125	200	6
6162 -60 ALASKA RAILROAD CABOOSE: 1959, unpainted yellow plastic with dark-blue with heat stamped markings..................		40	55	80	4
6167 LIONEL LINES CABOOSE: 1963-64.					
	Unpainted red........................	4	7	10	1
	Painted red.	60	100	175	6

6167 -85 Union Pacific Caboose

6167 -100 Lionel Lines Caboose

6167 -125 Undecorated Caboose

# Description	VG	EX	LN	S
6167 UNDECORATED CABOOSE: Unpainted olive drab.	200	375	550	7
6167 -25 UNDECORATED CABOOSE: 1963-64, red.	5	7	10	1
6167 -50 UNDECORATED CABOOSE: Unpainted yellow body.	12	20	35	4
6167 -85 UNION PACIFIC CABOOSE: 1963-66, 1969, unpainted yellow body black heat-stamped markings.	10	16	25	3
6167 -100 LIONEL LINES CABOOSE: 1963-64, unpainted red body.	5	10	14	2
6167 -125 UNDECORATED CABOOSE: 1963-64, unpainted red body.	5	7	10	1
6167 -150 LIONEL LINES CABOOSE: 1963-64, unpainted red body.	5	10	14	2
6167 -1967 T. T. O. S. HOPPER (Toy Train Operating Society): 1967, unpainted olive with metallic gold heat-stamped lettering.	50	65	100	6

6219 C&O Work Caboose

6220 A.T. & S.F. NW-2

6250 Seaboard NW-2

# Description	VG	EX	LN	S
6175 ROCKET FLAT CAR: 1958-61, white plastic rocket load heat-stamped "BUILT BY / LIONEL" and "U S NAVY" in blue.				
Unpainted red plastic.	40	60	85	4
Unpainted black plastic.	40	60	85	4
6176 LEHIGH VALLEY HOPPER: 1964-66, 1969.				
Bright yellow.	12	18	25	2
Dark yellow.	8	10	16	1
Gray.	8	10	16	1
Black.	10	15	20	2
6219 C&O WORK CABOOSE: 1960, tool compartment and cab painted dark blue.	30	50	75	5
6220 A.T. & S.F. NW-2: 1949-50, black, die-cast frame.				
With "6220" stamped on nose.	200	325	500	6
Without "6220" stamped on nose.	150	200	350	3
6250 SEABOARD NW-2: 1954-55, painted blue and orange.				
Decal "SEABOARD".	200	325	475	4
Rubber-stamped "SEABOARD" lettering.	500	675	950	6
Rubber-stamped, with wide spaced lettering (about 2 13/16 to 2 23/32 inches long.)	175	275	375	4
6257 LIONEL-SP CABOOSE: 1948-52.				
Painted red, red-orange or tile red.	2	5	8	1
Painted dark tile red, as was smokejack.	200	400	650	7

6262 Wheel Car, red

6262 Wheel Car, black

6264 Lumber Car

# Description	VG	EX	LN	S
6257X LIONEL-SP CABOOSE: 1948-only, tile-red painted equipped with TWO magnetic couplers rather than the usual one. The number 6247X appeared only on its original box. Because the car itself is easily replicated from a 6257, it MUST have its original box to realize the values shown..........................	15	25	35	5
6257 LIONEL CABOOSE: 1953-55.				
Unpainted red body....................	5	8	10	1
Painted red, tile red, or dark red...........	10	18	25	2
1956, double-circled L logo was eliminated. .	10	15	22	2
6257 -100 LIONEL LINES CABOOSE: 1963-64, unpainted red body, white heat-stamped lettering. Includes die-cast smokejack.......	15	25	40	4
6262 WHEEL CAR: 1956-57, originally furnished with six wheel and axle sets.				
Unpainted red body	400	1000	1500	7
Unpainted black body	50	75	100	4
6264 LUMBER CAR: 1957-58, unpainted red body came with 12 264-11 timbers retained by eight 2411-4 spring-steel posts.				
With bar-end metal trucks..............	30	50	75	5
With AAR-type trucks.................	40	65	90	6
6311 FLATCAR WITH PIPES: 1955 only, unpainted brown, cargo was three silver-gray plastic pipes, retained by six 2411-4 spring steel posts.	20	40	65	4

6315 Gulf Tank Car

6315 Lionel Lines Tank Car

6342 NYC Culvert Gondola

# Description	VG	EX	LN	S
6315 GULF TANK CAR: 1956-58. With flat burnt-orange bands painted on the ends.	25	55	80	2
Glossy burnt-orange paint.	50	95	150	5
Semi-gloss burnt-orange bands.	40	75	125	4
True orange bands.	60	125	175	5
6315 LIONEL LINES TANK CAR: 1963-66, all orange tank. Painted.	75	125	225	6
Unpainted.	10	20	40	3
6315 GULF: 1968-69. Unpainted orange tank. No "built date."	20	35	75	4
Rubber-stamped "BLT 1-56".	25	45	90	5
6342 NYC CULVERT GONDOLA: 1956-58, 1966-69. Dark red body marked "NEW 2-49", metal trucks..	15	25	40	4
Light red body; marked "NEW 2-49", AAR trucks.	15	25	40	3
Medium red body; no "NEW 2-49" markings, AAR trucks.	15	25	40	3
6343 BARREL RAMP CAR: 1961-62.	25	40	65	4
(6346) ALCOA COVERED HOPPER: 1956, painted silver, multi-colored ALCOA marking was adhesive-backed paper label.				
Heat-stamped blue lettering.	30	50	75	3
Black heat-stamped lettering.	125	175	250	6
Heat-stamped red lettering.	500	800	1300	7

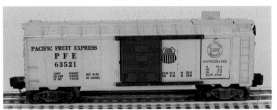

6352 Pacific Fruit Express Boxcar

6356 NYC Stock Car

6357 Lionel Caboose

# Description	VG	EX	LN	S
6352 PACIFIC FRUIT EXPRESS BOXCAR: 1955-57, unpainted orange body with black heat-stamped lettering.				
Four lines of data rubber-stamped on ice compartment door..	75	100	150	4
Three lines of data rubber-stamped on ice compartment door.	90	150	225	6
6356 NYC STOCK CAR: 1954-55, painted yellow.				
Rubber-stamped markings.	50	75	100	6
Heat stamped markings.	25	35	50	4
6357 LIONEL-SP CABOOSE: 1948-53.				
Painted red or tile red, without smokejack.	15	22	35	4
Tuscan or Maroon, with black die-cast smokejacks.	15	22	35	4
6357 LIONEL CABOOSE: 1953-61. Tuscan or Maroon, with black die-cast smokejacks.	15	22	35	4
Maroon body and maroon smokejack.	275	425	600	7
No double-circle Lionel "L" logo.	15	25	35	3
6357 -50 A.T.&S.F. CABOOSE: 1960-only, painted red with white heat-stamped markings.	600	1000	1800	8
6357 LIONEL CABOOSE: 1960-61. 1964-66, and 1968-69. Unpainted dark green body, stamped in dull-white, black-oxide chains.	40	70	100	4
Lighter green unlettered body, natural gold-color chain.	75	125	175	6

6362 Railway Truck Car

6376 Circus Stock Car

6402 Flatcar With Boat

#	Description	VG	EX	LN	S
6362 RAILWAY TRUCK CAR: 1955-57.					
Unpainted orange, shiny orange body bold serif lettering	30	45	70	4
Unpainted shiny with sans-serif lettering	30	45	70	4
Pale orange	125	175	250	7
6376 CIRCUS STOCK CAR: 1956-57, unpainted white plastic, with red trim and markings	60	100	150	5
6401 FLATCAR: 1965, unpainted gray body	2	5	10	1
6402 FLATCAR WITH REELS: 1962, 1964-66, 1969.					
Unpainted gray plastic body with orange or light gray reels	8	13	20	3
Brown plastic body with orange or light gray reels	8	13	20	3
6402 FLATCAR WITH BOAT: 1969, 6801-75 boat with blue hull	50	65	95	6
6404 FLATCAR WITH AUTOMOBILE: Black plastic body heat stamped "6404" and "BUILT BY LIONEL" in white.					
With yellow auto with gray bumpers	40	60	85	6
With red auto with gray bumpers	40	60	85	6
With a kelly green auto with gray bumpers	150	200	260	8
With dark brown auto with gray bumpers	150	200	260	8

NO LOAD (handwritten)

6405 Flatcar With Van

6407 Flatcar With Missile

6413 Mercury Capsule Carrying Car

#	Description	VG	EX	LN	S
6405 FLATCAR WITH VAN: 1961, heat-stamped "6405" furnished with a yellow plastic van with single rear wheels.	20	35	60	5
6406 FLATCAR WITH AUTO: 1961, gray or maroon plastic, unlettered flatcar carrying a single yellow automobile with gray bumpers..	50	75	100	6
6407 FLATCAR WITH MISSILE: 1963, with a large missile with removable Mercury capsule produced by Sterling Plastics. The Sterling Plastics name ALWAYS was molded into the base of the capsules.	300	500	700	7
6408 FLATCAR WITH PIPES: 1963, unpainted red plastic flatcar with five gray plastic pipes held on with a rubber band.	15	25	35	4
6409 -25 FLATCAR WITH PIPES: 1963, unpainted red plastic flatcar with three gray plastic pipes held on with a rubber band.	15	25	35	4
6411 FLATCAR: 1948-50, medium-gray flat car with three 7-inch long wooden 3/8-inch dowels.	20	30	40	3
6413 MERCURY CAPSULE CARRYING CAR: 1962-63.				
Unpainted blue body.	100	150	210	5
Painted blue..	150	200	300	6
Unpainted blue-green body.	300	400	600	8

6414 Evans Auto Loader

6414 Evans Auto Loader with Red Cars &
Gray Bumpers

6414 Evans Auto Loader with Kelly Green Cars &
Gray Bumpers

#	Description	VG	EX	LN	S
6414 EVANS AUTO LOADER: 1955-66, unpainted red body, black sheet metal superstructure. With four 4 5/16-inch long plastic automobiles.					
	Metal trucks and one each red, white, yellow and green automobiles.	75	110	165	4
	AAR-type trucks with one each red, white, yellow and green automobiles.	70	100	150	4
	"6414" to the left of "LIONEL", four red autos with gray bumpers.	100	150	200	5
	"6414" to the left of "LIONEL", four yellow autos with gray bumpers.	200	300	500	5
	"6414" to the left of "LIONEL", four kelly green autos with gray bumpers.	750	1000	1600	8
	"6414" to the left of "LIONEL", four brown autos with gray bumpers.	750	1000	1600	8
	Decaled "6414 AUTO LOADER" legend, four light red automobiles with gray bumpers.	200	400	650	8
6414 -85 EVANS AUTO LOADER: 1964 two yellow and two red automobiles adaptations from Lionel's slot cars with molded-in tires.		450	600	850	7
6415 SUNOCO TANK CAR: 1953-55, 1964-66, and 1969.					
	Capacity 6600 gallons, bar-end trucks.	10	17	30	3
	8000 gallons, bar-end trucks.	10	20	40	4
	6600 gallons, AAR-trucks.	10	20	40	4
6416 BOAT LOADER: 1961-63, with four boats with white-painted hulls, blue-painted cabin, and brown-painted interior.		125	175	250	5

RENKO CARS

6417 Pennsylvania Caboose

6417 -50 Lehigh Valley Caboose - Gray

6418 Machinery Car

#	Description	VG	EX	LN	S
6417 PENNSYLVANIA CABOOSE: 1953-57.					
Stamped "NEW YORK ZONE".........	20	30	45	3
Without "NEW YORK ZONE".........	200	300	425	7
6417 -25 LIONEL LINES CABOOSE: 1954-only.	20	30	55	3
6417 -50 LEHIGH VALLEY CABOOSE: 1954-					
only. Painted gray......................	75	125	175	5
Painted Tuscan red	600	1000	1600	8
6418 MACHINERY CAR: 1955-57.					
With two unnumbered black plastic girders with "LIONEL" in raised white letters.	75	100	125	4
With two unnumbered orange plastic girders with "LIONEL" in raised white lettering. ...	90	115	150	5
Orange girders with "LIONEL" in raised black lettering..............................	75	100	125	4
Orange girders without the raised "LIONEL" having accent color......................	75	100	125	4
Unnumbered orange plastic girders painted light gray..............................	90	115	150	5
Girders pinkish red-oxide primer color with raised "U.S. STEEL" lettering outlined in black.................................	90	115	150	5
Girders black with raised "U.S. STEEL" lettering outlined in white...............	75	100	125	4
6419 D. L & W. CABOOSE: 1948-50, 1952-55. .	25	35	50	3
6419 -25 D.L.&W. CABOOSE: 1954-55, bar-end trucks but only one coupler..............	25	35	50	4

6419 -100 N & W Caboose

6424 Twin Auto Car

6427 Lionel Lines Caboose

#	Description	VG	EX	LN	S
6419 -50 D. L. & W. CABOOSE: 1956-57, short die-cast smokejack, bar-end trucks and two magnetic couplers.	25	40	60	4
6419 -75 D. L. & W. CABOOSE: 1956, identical to the 6419-50, but with one coupler.	25	40	60	4
6419 -100 N & W CABOOSE: 1957-58.	100	150	250	6
6420 D. L. & W. CABOOSE: 1948-50, dark gray, with operating searchlight.	60	100	150	4
6424 TWIN AUTO CAR: 1956-59, unpainted black plastic, with automobiles with chrome bumpers. With bar-end metal trucks, "6424" heat-stamped to the right of the lettering. . .	30	50	75	4
AAR-type trucks, 6424" heat-stamped to the right of the lettering.	30	50	75	4
AAR-type trucks, 6424" heat-stamped to the left of Lionel.	30	50	75	4
Made with body tooling for the 6805 Radioactive Waste car.	175	300	425	8
6425 GULF TANK CAR: 1956-58.	15	30	50	3
6427 LIONEL LINES CABOOSE: 1954-60, numbered "64273".	20	30	45	3
6427 -60 VIRGINIAN CABOOSE: 1958, painted dark blue with yellow heat-stamped lettering.	125	250	450	6

6429 D. L. & W. Caboose

6430 Cooper-Jarrett Van Car

6436 Lehigh Valley Hopper

#	Description	VG	EX	LN	S
6427 -500 PENNSYLVANIA CABOOSE: 1957-58, painted sky blue and decorated with white heat-stamped lettering, including the number "576427".............................		200	350	525	6
6428 UNITED STATES MAIL BOXCAR: 1960-61, 1965-66.		20	35	50	3
6429 D. L. & W. CABOOSE: 1963-only.........		150	275	450	7
6430 COOPER-JARRETT VAN CAR: 1956-58, unpainted red flatcar with vans............		45	70	100	4
6431 PIGGY-BACK CAR WITH TRAILER TRUCKS AND TRACTOR: 1966, packaged with two trailers and a road tractor. Car heat-stamped 6430, the 6431 number appearing exclusively on the end of the original box....		175	250	375	7
6434 POULTRY DISPATCH STOCK CAR: 1958-59, painted red, illuminated..............		45	70	100	4
6436 LEHIGH VALLEY HOPPER: 1955-56, 1966, black open-top hopper.					
Marked "646361", without spreader bar......		50	65	90	6
Marked "646361" with spreader bar.........		20	35	50	4
Marked "643625" without spreader bar......		50	75	100	4
Marked "643625" with spreader bar.........		20	35	50	3

6436 -1969 T C A Hopper

6437 Pennsylvania Caboose

6440 Pullman

# Description	VG	EX	LN	S
6436 LEHIGH VALLEY HOPPER: 1963-68, red, cataloged as 6436-110.				
No spreader bar, stamped "NEW 3-55" on sides..	35	50	85	4
No spreader bar and no new date markings...	20	30	50	3
With spreader bar, and "NEW 3-55" on sides.	35	50	85	4
6436 LEHIGH VALLEY HOPPER: 1957-58, lilac painted, with maroon heat-stamped lettering numbered "643657"..				
Without spreader bar.	325	500	800	6
With spreader.	150	250	375	4
6436 -1969 T C A HOPPER (Train Collectors Association): 1969	75	90	125	4
6437 PENNSYLVANIA CABOOSE: 1961-68...	17	25	40	3
6440 PULLMAN: 1948-49, brown sheet metal...	25	40	70	3
6440 FLATCAR WITH PIGGY-BACK VANS: 1961-63 Red flatcar with unpainted gray plastic trailers with only single rear wheels and no decoration.	60	100	140	5
6441 OBSERVATION: 1948-49, brown sheet metal.	25	35	60	3
6442 PULLMAN: 1949, brown sheet metal......	30	60	90	3

GREEN (handwritten)

NO LWAS (handwritten)

CREEN (handwritten)

6445 Fort Knox Gold Reserve

6446 N & W Covered Hopper

6446 (-25) N & W

#	Description	VG	EX	LN	S
6443 OBSERVATION: 1949, brown sheet metal..		30	60	90	3
6445 FORT KNOX GOLD RESERVE: 1961-63.		80	125	175	5
6446 N & W COVERED HOPPER: 1954-55, Gray-painted body with cover, without spreader-brace holes, marked "546446"......		30	45	60	3
Black-painted body with cover, without spreader-brace holes, marked "546446"......		30	45	60	3
Black-painted body with cover, with spreader-brace holes, marked "546446".		50	85	140	5
6446 (-25) N & W: 1955-57, 1963. Gray-painted body with cover, and without spreader bar holes, marked "644625".......		25	40	60	3
Gray-painted body with cover, with spreader bar holes, marked "644625".............		45	65	110	5
Black-painted body with cover, without spreader bar holes, marked "644625".		25	40	60	3
Unpainted gray plastic body which had spreader-bar holes, marked "644625", AAR trucks.		80	125	180	6
6446 LEHIGH VALLEY HOPPER (6446-60): 1963, body painted red, roof and hatches unpainted red.		110	175	275	7
6447 PENNSYLVANIA CABOOSE: 1963 only...		200	325	500	7

X6454 A.T.&S.F. Boxcar

X6454 N Y C Boxcar

X6454 N Y C Boxcar

# Description	VG	EX	LN	S
6448 TARGET RANGE BOXCAR: 1961-64.				
Red roof and ends and white side panels..	18	25	40	4
White roof and ends and red side panels. ...	18	25	40	4
6452 PENNSYLVANIA GONDOLA: 1948-49.				
Numbered "6462" on side and rubber-stamped				
"6452" on bottom of the frame	12	16	25	3
car side numbered "6452"...............	12	16	25	3
X6454 A.T.&S.F. BOXCAR: 1948, painted orange				
with black markings..................	25	40	60	5
X6454 BABY RUTH BOXCAR: 1948, painted				
light orange	125	250	375	7
X6454 ERIE BOXCAR: 1949-52, brown with				
white markings......................	30	45	70	4
X6454 N Y C BOXCAR: 1948-only.				
Tan body with white lettering	20	30	45	3
Brown body with white lettering	30	50	75	4
Orange body lettered in black	75	125	200	7
X6454 PENNSYLVANIA BOXCAR: 1949-52				
brown................................	30	45	70	4

6456 Lehigh Valley, red

6460 Bucyrus Erie Crane, black

6460 Bucyrus Erie Crane, red

# Description	VG	EX	LN	S
X6454 SOUTHERN PACIFIC BOXCAR: 1949-52, brown.				
Short piece of the outer circle of the Southern Pacific logo missing between the "R" and the "N".	50	75	125	6
Broken circle was fixed.	30	45	70	4
6456 LEHIGH VALLEY: 1948-55.				
Painted black.	8	10	15	1
Painted dull maroon.	8	10	15	1
Painted semi-gloss maroon.	18	25	35	3
Painted gray body.	25	40	55	4
Painted glossy red with white heat-stamped markings.	350	500	800	7
Painted glossy red with yellow heat-stamped markings.	75	110	175	5
6457 LIONEL CABOOSE: 1949-52.				
Tuscan-painted body and matching plastic smokejack.	20	30	45	2
Tuscan-painted with matching die-cast smokejack.	15	25	35	1
Tuscan or maroon painted bodies with black die-cast smokejack.	15	25	35	1
6460 BUCYRUS ERIE CRANE: 1952-54.				
Black.	40	75	95	3
Red.	40	75	125	4
6461 TRANSFORMER CAR: 1949-50, gray die-cast flatcar with black transformer load.	50	75	100	4

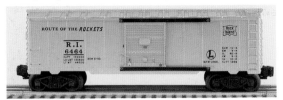

6464-1 Western Pacific Boxcar

6464-25 Great Northern Boxcar

6464 -50 Minneapolis & St. Louis

# Description	VG	EX	LN	S
6462 NEW YORK CENTRAL GONDOLA: 1949-56.				
Painted black	10	13	16	1
Unpainted black body	8	10	12	1
Painted tile red.	8	12	15	1
True red painted (not the tile red)	20	28	40	4
Red-orange painted	10	15	20	3
Unpainted red	10	15	20	3
Painted green	15	22	32	3
6462 -500 NEW YORK CENTRAL GONDOLA: 1957-58, Pink	150	200	300	5
6463 ROCKET FUEL TANK CAR: 1962-63, painted snow-white with bright red rubber-stamped lettering	15	25	60	4
6464 -1 WESTERN PACIFIC BOXCAR: 1953-54, painted silver ribs on inside of roof.				
Lettering heat-stamped in blue	600	850	1400	7
Red heat-stamped markings	975	1600	2500	8
Smooth interior of the roof, blue markings . .	55	85	110	3
6464 -25 GREAT NORTHERN BOXCAR: 1953-54, painted orange with white heat-stamped lettering	60	75	100	3

6464 -75 Rock Island

6464 -100 Western Pacific

6464 -125 Pacemaker Boxcar

6464 -150 Missouri Pacific Boxcar

#	Description	VG	EX	LN	S
6464 -50 MINNEAPOLIS & ST LOUIS: 1953-56. Four full columns of rivets to the right of the door	50	70	100	3
Three full columns of rivets to the right of the door	750	1250	2100	8
6464 -75 ROCK ISLAND: 1953-54, 1969, green-painted body	60	80	100	3
6464 -100 WESTERN PACIFIC: 1954-55, silver (see 6464-250 for orange)	100	130	190	5
6464 -125 PACEMAKER BOXCAR: 1954-56, red and gray decorated with white	75	110	150	5
6464 -150 MISSOURI PACIFIC BOXCAR: 1954-55, 1957. "Eagle" and "NEW 3 54" were stamped to the right of the door. Single tack board doors with gray stripes were installed on this car	75	125	160	4
"NEW 3 54" stamped to the left of the door .	75	125	160	4
Masking of the blue and gray stripes. The single tack block doors solid yellow. "NEW 3 54" stamped to the left of the door.	75	125	160	4
Circular Missouri Pacific Lines herald stamped in the panel immediately to the left of the door; all the other cars have this herald in the fourth panel from the left end of the car	850	1250	2000	8
"Eagle" and the circular Missouri Pacific herald noticeably smaller	75	125	160	4

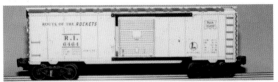

6464 -175 Rock Island

6464 -200 Pennsylvania Boxcar

6464 -225 Southern Pacific Boxcar

6464 -250 Western Pacific Boxcar

# Description	VG	EX	LN	S
6464 -175 ROCK ISLAND: 1954-55, painted silver. Markings heat-stamped in blue, four columns of rivets to right of door.	75	110	175	5
Heat-stamped lettering in black	750	1000	1650	8
Three full columns of rivets to the right of the door, lettered in blue	800	1250	2100	8
6464 -200 PENNSYLVANIA BOXCAR: 1954-55, 1969, Tuscan-painted doors and body	75	110	150	5
6464 -225 SOUTHERN PACIFIC BOXCAR: 1954-56. Second column of rivets from the left end of the car has two interruptions	750	1200	2100	8
Second rivet column has only five rivets	75	110	150	4
6464 -250 WESTERN PACIFIC BOXCAR: 1954, 1966, painted orange with a blue rubber-stamped feather and white rubber-stamped lettering				
Second rivet column to the left of the door had five rivets, three at the top and two at the bottom	500	1000	1600	8
Second and third rivet columns each had five rivets	130	200	275	5
Erroneously stamped 6464-100	700	1000	1300	8

6464-275 State Of Maine Boxcar

6464-300 Rutland Boxcar

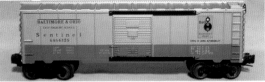

6464-325 Baltimore & Ohio Sentinel Boxcar

6464 -350 M-K-T (Missouri-Kansas-Texas) Boxcar

#	Description	VG	EX	LN	S
6464 -275 STATE OF MAINE BOXCAR: 1955, 1957-59.					
	Unpainted white body with grooves, doors unpainted red plastic	100	165	250	6
	Unpainted royal blue body with grooves, doors painted white plastic	90	150	210	5
	Grooved body painted all three colors, doors painted white plastic	60	90	125	4
	No grooves	60	90	125	4
6464 -300 RUTLAND BOXCAR: 1955-56.					
	Clear body casting painted green and yellow .	500	750	1100	7
	Rutland herald has a solid dark green background	2000	2700	4000	8
	Molded yellow body, herald with yellow background	75	125	175	4
	Lower half of doors painted glossy dark green	650	1000	1500	7
	Faint outline of 6352 roof top hatch visible . .	450	675	900	6
6464 -325 BALTIMORE & OHIO SENTINEL BOXCAR: 1956 only. Painted silver, and aqua.					
	Single tack board doors	500	700	975	7
	Multiple tack boards	400	625	875	6
6464 -350 M-K-T (Missouri-Kansas-Texas) BOXCAR: 1956-only	200	300	400	5

6464-375 Central Of Georgia Boxcar

464-400 Baltimore & Ohio Boxcar

6464-425 New Haven Boxcar

# Description	VG	EX	LN	S
6464 -375 CENTRAL OF GEORGIA BOXCAR: 1956-57, 1966.				
The interior of the roof was smooth, decoration includes a built date of 3-56.	75	110	150	4
Interior of the roof ribbed, car does NOT have a "built date."	75	110	150	4
Interior of the roof ribbed markings include the "3-56" built date	1600	2250	3500	8
6464 -400 BALTIMORE & OHIO BOXCAR: 1956-57, 1969.				
Marked "BLT 5-54 BY LIONEL".	70	115	160	4
Marked "BLT 2-56 BY LIONEL".	155	225	300	6
Marked "BLT 5-54 BY LIONEL" on one side and "BLT 2-56 BY LIONEL" on the other. .	500	850	1400	8
No built date information stamped on.	70	100	150	4
6464 -425 NEW HAVEN BOXCAR: 1956-58.				
Unpainted black body, "N" of the NH logo had only a half serif on top right corner.	40	60	80	3
Unpainted black body, "N" of the NH logo had full serif	40	60	80	3
Matte-black painted body, "N" of the NH logo had half serif on the top right corner	40	60	80	3
Matte-black painted body, "N" of the NH logo had a full serif	40	60	80	3
Painted glossy black, "N" of the NH logo a half serif	40	60	80	3

6464 -450 Great Northern Boxcar

6464 -475 Boston And Maine Boxcar

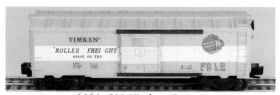

6464 -500 Timken Boxcar

#	Description	VG	EX	LN	S

6464 -450 GREAT NORTHERN BOXCAR: 1956-57, 1966, painted olive with broad horizontal orange stripe with yellow delineating stripes, interior of the roof smooth.

		VG	EX	LN	S
Lettered "BLT 1-56 BY LIONEL"		75	125	175	4
The interior of the roof was ribbed. Lettered "BLT 1-56 BY LIONEL"		400	600	900	8
Lettered "BLT BY LIONEL", no date stamped.		75	125	175	4

6464 -475 BOSTON AND MAINE BOXCAR: 1957-60, 1965-68. Interior of roof smooth, stamped "BLT 2-57 BY LIONEL" . . . .

		VG	EX	LN	S
stamped "BLT 2-57 BY LIONEL"		35	50	65	3
Interior of roof ribbed, stamped "BLT 2-57 BY LIONEL".		35	50	65	3
Second rivet column to the left of the door had five rivets, no date, only "BLT BY LIONEL".		35	50	65	3
No built date stamped, second and third rivet columns each only five rivets		75	150	200	6
Second and third rivet columns each only five rivets, stamped "BLT 2-57 BY LIONEL" . . .		65	125	175	5

6464 -500 TIMKEN BOXCAR: 1957-59, 1969. Yellow, or yellow-orange plastic, stamped "BLT 3-57 BY LIONEL", smooth roof interior. . . . .

		VG	EX	LN	S
interior.		75	125	175	4
Gray plastic, painted both yellow and white, stamped "BLT 3-57 BY LIONEL", smooth roof interior		300	275	425	6
Ribbed roof interior, stamped "BLT 3-57 BY LIONEL".		150	200	275	5
Ribbed roof interior, no built date		75	125	175	4

6464-510 Pacemaker & 6464-15 M-K-T Boxcars

6464 -525 Minneapolis & St Louis Boxcar

6464 -650 Rio Grande Boxcar

6464 -700 Santa Fe Boxcar

#	Description	VG	EX	LN	S
6464 -510 PACEMAKER BOXCAR: 1957-58, pastel blue		500	675	950	7
6464 -515 M-K-T BOXCAR: 1957-58 pastel yellow................................		500	675	950	7
6464 -525 MINNEAPOLIS & ST LOUIS BOXCAR: 1957-58, 1964-66.					
Molded in red plastic, painted red, smooth roof interior		35	60	100	4
White or marbleized red plastic painted red, ribbed roof interior....................		35	60	100	4
Gray plastic painted red.................		35	60	100	4
6464 -650 RIO GRANDE BOXCAR: 1957-58, 1966.					
Unpainted yellow body molding with silver painted on, including roof, heat stamped "BLT 6-57 BY LIONEL"		75	125	175	4
Unpainted yellow body molding with silver painted on, including roof, heat stamped "BLT BY LIONEL".........................		75	125	175	4
Gray body casting, with both yellow and silver painted on, roof painted yellow		1100	1600	2800	8
6464 -700 SANTA FE BOXCAR: 1961,1966.					
To left of door, the second rivet column had only five rivets		950	1500	2500	8
The second and third left rivet columns each had only five rivets		80	125	185	4

6464 -725 New Haven Boxcar

6464 -825 Alaska Railroad Boxcar

6464 -900 New York Central Boxcar

#	Description	VG	EX	LN	S
6464 -725 NEW HAVEN BOXCAR: 1962-66, 1968-69. Orange, with black door		45	60	100	3
	Black, with orange door	200	275	375	5
6464 -825 ALASKA RAILROAD BOXCAR: 1959-60, doors of authentic cars are always blue.					
Left of the door, second rivet column had only five rivets		175	275	375	5
Second and third rivet columns to the left of the door each had only five rivets		250	375	550	6
6464 -900 NEW YORK CENTRAL BOXCAR: 1960-66, body painted jade green.					
Green doors, left of the door, second rivet column had only five rivets		900	1350	2200	8
Green doors, second and third rivet columns to the left of the door each had only five rivets		75	125	175	4
Light jade green with unpainted black multiple tack board doors.		60	110	150	6
6464 -1965 TRAIN COLLECTORS ASSOCIATION BOXCAR: 1965, uncataloged commemorative for the 1965 TCA convention in Pittsburgh, painted blue body.		80	200	250	8
6465 SUNOCO TANK CAR: 1948-56, two-dome painted silver.					
Technical data ends with the word "TANK" .		5	10	15	1
Distinct gray cast		15	20	35	4
Last line of technical data ends with "6465". .		10	15	25	4

6465 Gulf/Lionel Lines Tank Car

6465 Gulf/Lionel Lines Tank Car

6465 Lionel Lines Tank Car

# Description	VG	EX	LN	S
6465 GULF/LIONEL LINES TANK CAR: 1958. Unpainted gray plastic with the lettering rubber-stamped in blue	15	18	25	3
Molded black body and white rubber-stamped lettering	40	55	85	4
Painted black with white rubber stamped lettering	50	75	100	5
6465 LIONEL LINES TANK CAR: 1959, 1963-66. Unpainted black body with white rubber-stamped lettering	15	40	55	4
Orange	4	8	12	1
6465 CITIES SERVICE TANK CAR: 1960-62, painted green	15	25	35	3
6467 MISCELLANEOUS FLATCAR: 1956-only, molded red plastic body white heat-stamped "LIONEL 6467". Unpainted black plastic bulkhead, four spring-steel 2411-4 posts, no load furnished	30	45	70	4
6468 BALTIMORE & OHIO BOXCAR: 1953-55. Painted blue, either glossy or flat	40	65	100	4
Painted Tuscan	250	350	475	7

6468 -25 New Haven Boxcar

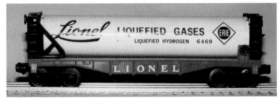

6469 Liquefied Gas Car

6472 Refrigerator

#	Description	VG	EX	LN	S
6468 -25 NEW HAVEN BOXCAR: 1956-58, orange body, black doors, "N" of the New Haven logo stamped in black. The "N" sometimes appears with a full serif, other times with a half serif, but both are equally common		50	75	110	4
Half-serif "N" of the logo heat stamped in white.		150	225	325	6
Tuscan doors		NOT LEGITIMATE			
6469 LIQUEFIED GAS CAR: 1963-only. Unpainted red plastic with orange tint, heat-stamped "Lionel" in white, black molded plastic bulkheads glued in place. The load was a cardboard tube wrapped in glossy white paper. On it, printed in black, was the car number "6469" and an Erie herald. Sheet-metal caps were painted white and crimped on each end of the tube		40	90	140	5
6470 EXPLOSIVES BOXCAR: 1959-60		30	50	70	4
6472 REFRIGERATOR: 1950-53		25	35	50	4
6473 HORSE TRANSPORT CAR: 1962-66, 1969.		25	35	50	3
6475 PICKLES : 1960-62. Without the hoop and stave stamping, but with the red "Pickles" . . .		35	50	85	4
With hoop and stave stamping, and "Pickles" lettering.		25	45	65	3

6475 Libby's Crushed Pineapple

6476 Lehigh Valley Hopper

6476 Lehigh Valley

#	Description	VG	EX	LN	S
6475 LIBBY'S CRUSHED PINEAPPLE: 1963–64, vats covered in adhesive silver paper with Libby's logos. Aqua body		50	60	85	4
Medium-blue body		30	40	60	3
6476 LEHIGH VALLEY HOPPER: 1957-69, early 1957 production equipped with metal trucks, remainder of the production used AAR trucks. Red		10	16	22	2
Gray		10	16	22	2
Black		10	16	22	2
6476-1 TOY TRAIN OPERATING SOCIETY HOPPER: 1969 only, uncataloged		40	65	110	5
6476 LEHIGH VALLEY: 1959-63. Medium red opaque body		8	10	15	1
Light translucent red body		8	10	15	1
Dark translucent red body		8	10	15	1
Coral-pink opaque body		15	30	50	4
Black		15	25	45	4
6476 -135 LEHIGH VALLEY: 1964-66, 1968, listed in various catalogs was a yellow 6476 hopper. Be advised, however, that no yellow hopper cars were produced with the numbered "6476" stamped on them. Rather, the 6476 number denoted two operating couplers. The cars themselves used various black Lehigh Valley heat stamps, with various numbers and built and new dates		SEE OTHER LISTINGS			

6480 Explosives Boxcar

6482 Refrigerator

6500 Beechcraft Bonanza Transport Car

#	Description	VG	EX	LN	S

6477 MISCELLANEOUS CAR WITH PIPES:
1957-58, molded red plastic body with
unpainted black plastic bulkheads and four
spring-steel 2411-4 posts, with a load of five
silver-gray plastic pipes **30**   **60**   **80**   **4**

6480 EXPLOSIVES BOXCAR: 1961-only **30**   **50**   **70**   **4**

6482 REFRIGERATOR: 1957-only, always had
sprung plastic doors **40**   **55**   **85**   **5**

**6500 BEECHCRAFT BONANZA TRANSPORT
CAR**: 1962, unnumbered, unpainted black
flatcar. Airplane secured using a 6418-9
elastic band. Airplane heat-stamped with
"BONANZA" on each side and the FAA
registration number N2742B on one wing.
Lionel New York identification molded into
underside of the fuselage. Four rivets bind each
wing together.

White lettering, red upper wings and fuselage.
The lower fuselage half and propeller were
white **425**   **550**   **750**   **6**
It had white upper surfaces, red lower surfaces
and a red propeller **550**   **700**   **950**   **7**

6501 FLATCAR WITH MOTORBOAT: 1962-63,
with small plastic boat that was propelled
through the water by pellets of baking soda,
supplied with the car in a foil packet of 40 . .   **90**   **125**   **175**   **5**

6502 Steel Girder Transport Car

6511 Pipe Car

6511 Pipe Car

# Description	VG	EX	LN	S
6502 STEEL GIRDER TRANSPORT CAR: 1962-63, with a single unpainted orange girder with "LIONEL" in raised lettering retained by a 6418-9 elastic band.				
Unpainted black plastic body.............	20	35	60	5
Unpainted red plastic body	50	80	125	6
6502 -50 STEEL GIRDER TRANSPORT CAR: Circa 1963, unlettered, unpainted blue plastic car payload was single unpainted orange girder with "LIONEL" in raised lettering retained by a 6418-9 elastic band..................	25	40	60	5
6511 PIPE CAR: 1953-56, furnished with five standard silver-gray plastic pipes and a small envelope containing 13 2411-4 spring steel posts.				
Molded of black plastic painted dark red. Die-cast plates on the underside of each end of the car served as attachment points for the trucks....................	25	50	75	5
Painted a dull brick red with die-cast plates....................	25	50	75	5
Painted dark red with blued-steel plates	20	40	60	3
Unpainted light brown body with blued-steel plates....................	20	45	65	4
Unpainted reddish brown with blued-steel plates....................	20	40	60	3
6512 CHERRY PICKER CAR: 1962-63	75	100	150	5

6517 -75 Erie Caboose

6518 Transformer Car

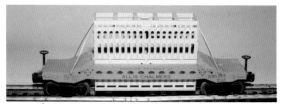

6519 Allis-Chalmers Heat Exchanger Car

#	Description	VG	EX	LN	S
6517 LIONEL LINES CABOOSE: 1955-59. Underscoring beneath "BLT 12-55" and "LIONEL".	45	75	100	5
No underscoring	40	60	80	4
6517 -75 ERIE CABOOSE: 1966-only	250	400	525	7
6517 /1966 TCA CABOOSE: 1966 uncataloged commemorative	75	125	200	7
6518 TRANSFORMER CAR: 1956-58, upper transformer panel heat-stamped in white "6518", lower panel was heat stamped "LIONEL TRANSFORMER CAR".	75	115	155	5
6519 ALLIS-CHALMERS HEAT EXCHANGER CAR: 1958-61.				
Molded medium orange plastic	55	85	125	4
Dark orange plastic	55	85	125	4
Milky-orange colored plastic	100	140	200	6
6520 LIONEL LINES: 1949-51, simulated generator hid an off-on switch that could be actuated with a remote control uncoupling track. Beware of reproduction generators.				
Tan generator.	300	550	750	8
Green generator.	225	350	475	6
Orange generator	35	50	75	3
Maroon generator	50	75	100	4

6530 Firefighting Instruction Car

6555 Sunoco Tank Car

6556 M-K-T Stock Car

# Description	VG	EX	LN	S
6530 FIREFIGHTING INSTRUCTION CAR: 1960-62, unpainted red plastic body and unpainted white plastic opening doors.	65	100	150	5
6536 M & St. L HOPPER: (Minneapolis & St. Louis) 1958-59, 1963, large open-topped hopper.	35	55	85	4
6544 MISSILE FIRING CAR: 1960-64, came with two small envelopes, each containing four 44-40 rockets. Control panel heat-stamped in white	100	140	225	4
Control panel heat-stamped in black.	225	375	550	6
6555 SUNOCO TANK CAR: 1949-50, tank painted silver. Sunoco decal with "GAS" above and "OILS" below "SUNOCO" in the herald	20	40	65	4
Without the "GAS / OILS" in the herald . . .	20	40	65	4
6556 M-K-T STOCK CAR: 1958-only.	150	250	450	7
6557 LIONEL SMOKING CABOOSE: 1958-59. 6557 stamped on the left end of the car.	150	250	400	6
6557 stamped on the right-hand end of the body.	200	350	550	7

6560 Bucyrus Erie Crane

656025 Bucyrus Erie Crane

6561 Cable Reel Car

# Description	VG	EX	LN	S
6560 BUCYRUS ERIE CRANE: 1955-64, 1966-69.				
Equipped with metal trucks mounted using binding head screws and spacer rings.	100	175	250	5
Gray cab, no spacer rings, metal trucks, crank wheels with open spokes	60	80	110	4
Molded red cab, open spoke crank wheels, metal trucks	30	45	60	3
Red cab, no number on frame, metal trucks, open spoke crank wheels	50	70	90	4
Red cab, AAR-type trucks, open spoke crank wheels	30	45	65	3
Red cab, AAR-type trucks, solid crank wheels	30	45	65	3
Red cab, dark blue frame	50	75	100	4
656025 BUCYRUS ERIE CRANE: 1956, red cab, frame heat-stamped 656025	65	105	140	5
6561 CABLE REEL CAR: 1953-56. Reels wound with solid aluminum wire.				
Gray unpainted plastic reels.	55	85	110	5
Unpainted orange plastic reels	45	65	90	4
6562 NEW YORK CENTRAL GONDOLA: 1956-58, usually included a load of four red canisters with "Lionel Air Activated Container" lettering.				
Gray.	28	45	60	4
Red	28	45	60	4
Black	28	45	60	4

6572 Railway Express Agency Refrigerator

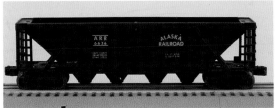

6636 Alaska Railroad Hopper

6640 U.S.M.C. Missile Launching Car

#	Description	VG	EX	LN	S
6572 RAILWAY EXPRESS AGENCY REFRIGERATOR: 1958-59, 1963. Painted dark green and equipped with 2400-series passenger car trucks		85	135	200	6
Bar-end metal trucks		80	125	175	5
Light green with AAR-type trucks		65	95	125	4
6630 MISSILE LAUNCHING CAR: 1961, unpainted black plastic body with pivoting blue plastic launcher base		75	110	165	5
6636 ALASKA RAILROAD HOPPER: 1959-60		35	55	85	4
6640 U.S.M.C. MISSILE LAUNCHING CAR: 1960 Body painted olive drab and was heat-stamped "U.S.M.C. 6640" in white. Unpainted olive drab plastic launcher base with a black plastic launch rail		150	225	325	7
6646 LIONEL LINES STOCK CAR: 1957 only. Orange		25	35	55	5
6650 MISSILE LAUNCHING CAR: 1959-63, unpainted red plastic body heat-stamped "6650 LIONEL". Pivoting unpainted blue plastic launcher base with a black plastic launch rail		35	50	75	4
6651 U.S. MARINE CORPS CANNON FIRING CAR: 1964-65		125	225	300	6

REPRO LOAD

6656 Lionel Lines Stock Car

6657 Rio Grande Caboose

6672 Santa Fe Refrigerator

#	Description	VG	EX	LN	S
6656 LIONEL LINES STOCK CAR: 1950-53.					
Bright yellow with adhesive-backed "Armour" emblem applied to the doors	50	75	100	5
Bright yellow without "Armour" emblem. . . .	18	25	35	3
Dark yellow without "Armour" emblem.	18	25	35	3
6657 RIO GRANDE CABOOSE: 1957-58.					
Body molded with slots in the roof overhang to accept ladders, which were not installed . .	75	125	200	5
Body molded without the ladder slots	125	200	375	7
6660 BOOM CAR: 1958, equipped with a pair of outriggers.	50	75	115	5
6670 DERRICK CAR: 1959-60, no outriggers . . .	40	60	90	4
6672 SANTA FE REFRIGERATOR: 1954-56.					
Three lines of data to the right of the door and blue heat-stamped lettering	150	250	425	7
Either black or blue lettering with two lines of data to right of door.	45	75	100	4
Black-lettering, no circled-L Lionel logo. . . .	45	75	100	4
6736 DETROIT & MACKINAC HOPPER: 1960-62.					
Face of the figure in Mackinac Mac clear . . .	25	45	65	3
Face of Mackinac Mac partially obliterated . .	25	45	65	3

6800 Airplane Car

6800 Airplane Car

6801 Boat Car

# Description	VG	EX	LN	S

6800 AIRPLANE CAR: 1957-60, unpainted red flatcar, undecorated yellow and black plastic aircraft with identifying markings molded into the underside of the fuselage. These markings read, "NO. 6800-60 AIRPLANE THE LIONEL CORPORATION NEW YORK, N.Y. MADE IN U.S. OF AMERICA". Either black upper surfaces and yellow propeller or yellow upper surfaces with black propeller. Only three rivets to bind the wing halves.

Car equipped with metal trucks. 150 200 300 5

Equipped with AAR-type trucks, number stamped to the right of "LIONEL" 150 200 300 5

Equipped with AAR-type trucks, number stamped to the left of "LIONEL" 150 200 300 5

6801 BOAT CAR: 1957-60, unpainted red flatcar with boat secured in an unpainted gray plastic cradle by 6418-9 elastic band.

Metal trucks, white-hulled boat with a brown deck that had no Lionel markings. 70 100 150 4

AAR-type trucks, white-hulled boat with a brown deck that had no Lionel markings . . . 70 100 150 4

6801-50 BOAT CAR: AAR-type trucks, boat with yellow hull marked "NO. 6801-60 BOAT MADE IN U.S. OF AMERICA" to the right of the engine hatch and "THE LIONEL CORPORATION NEW YORK, N.Y.". . . . 70 100 150 4

6803 Flatcar with Military Units

6804 Flatcar with Military Units

6805 Radioactive Waste Car

#	Description	VG	EX	LN	S
6801 -75 BOAT CAR: AAR-type trucks, boat with blue hull marked "NO. 6801-60 BOAT MADE IN U.S. OF AMERICA" to the right of the engine hatch and "THE LIONEL CORPORATION NEW YORK, N.Y." on the left	70	100	150	4
6802 FLATCAR WITH GIRDERS: 1958-59 molded red flatcar with two black plastic "U.S. STEEL" girders secured with a 6418-9 elastic band. Car heat-stamped "6802 LIONEL" . . .	20	25	35	4
6803 FLATCAR WITH MILITARY UNITS: 1958-59, Hauled a tank and a truck with swiveling loudspeakers, both heat-stamped with US Marine Corps markings.	125	200	300	6
6804 FLATCAR WITH MILITARY UNITS: 1958-59, one truck with swiveling twin antiaircraft guns and a second truck with swiveling loudspeakers. USMC markings on vehicles . .	125	200	300	6
6805 RADIOACTIVE WASTE CAR: 1958-59, with two illuminated painted gray simulated concrete radioactive waste containers.	75	125	175	5
6806 FLATCAR WITH MILITARY UNITS: 1958-59, cargo was a medical truck and a truck with a swiveling radar antenna.	100	175	275	6

6807 Flatcar with DUKW

6808 Flatcar with Military Load

6809 Flatcar with Military Units

#	Description	VG	EX	LN	S
6807 FLATCAR WITH DUKW: 1958-59, cargo was amphibious 2 1/2 ton 6x6 truck	75	100	150	5
6808 FLATCAR WITH MILITARY LOAD: 1958-59, carried a truck with a searchlight and a replica of a M19 Gun Motor Carriage with twin 40mm Bofors antiaircraft cannon	200	275	400	6
6809 FLATCAR WITH MILITARY UNITS: 1958-59, carried a medical van and truck with swiveling twin antiaircraft guns	125	200	300	6
6810 FLATCAR WITH COOPER-JARRETT VAN: 1958, carried one white trailer with black and copper-colored Cooper-Jarrett signs	35	50	70	5

6812 Track Maintenance Car

6812 Track Maintenance Car

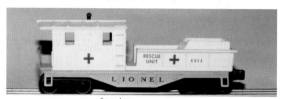

6814 Rescue Unit

#	Description	VG	EX	LN	S
6812 TRACK MAINTENANCE CAR: 1959-61, body unpainted red plastic heat-stamped "6812" to the left of "LIONEL" in white serif letters.					
All three plastic components of their superstructure molded in matching black plastic.	50	80	125	4
Black superstructure base with a gray platform and crank handle	50	80	125	4
Gray superstructure base with black platform and crank handle	50	80	125	4
All three superstructure components molded gray plastic.	50	80	125	4
All three superstructure components molded bright lemon yellow plastic	50	80	125	4
All three superstructure components molded dark yellow plastic	80	125	150	5
All three superstructure components molded of cream-colored plastic.	100	200	275	7
6814 RESCUE UNIT: 1959-61, referred to by the catalog as a First Aid Medical Car, it included a tool compartment insert, two molded plastic stretchers, and oxygen tank and a blue rubber figure. All the plastic components were painted white with red heat-stamped markings, including red crosses on the stretchers. The sheet-metal frame was painted gray.	50	100	165	5

6816 Flatcar with Allis-Chalmers Crawler Tractor

6816 Flatcar with Allis-Chalmers Crawler Tractor

#	Description	VG	EX	LN	S

6816 FLATCAR WITH ALLIS-CHALMERS CRAWLER TRACTOR: 1959-60. The earliest dozer ((Type I) was believed to have been molded in dark orange plastic. "ALLIS-CHALMERS" was heat-stamped on the back of the seat in white while the "TORQUE CONVERTER" emblem was heat stamped in black on each side of the seat. The raised "ALLIS-CHALMERS" molded alongside the hood was picked out in black.Lionel soon discontinued the black highlighting of the lettering on the hood, resulting in the first variation in the design. We will call this the Type II tractor. The next variation (Type III) came about when "HD 16 DIESEL" began to be stamped in black above the torque converter emblem on the seat sides. The Type IV was identical to the Type III, except the rear drawbar was shortened and its holes filled in. When production of the Type V tractor began, the seat back lettering was changed to black. The final version (Type VI) was made of a considerably lighter orange plastic than the other vehicles.In addition to being packaged with the flatcar, this bulldozer was also offered for separate sale by Lionel packaged in an orange picture box, and by Allis-Chalmers, which had it packed in a striped box. Most of these flatcars had unpainted red plastic bodies. If found with a Type I or Type VI dozer, a 50 percent premium should be added to the values shown here **300 475 650 6**

Unpainted black plastic bodies. Once again, a Type I or Type II dozer would increase the values shown **1000 1650 3000 8**

6817 Flatcar with Allis-Chalmers Scraper

6817 Flatcar with Allis-Chalmers Scraper

#	Description	VG	EX	LN	S

6817 FLATCAR WITH ALLIS-CHALMERS SCRAPER: 1959-60, with orange articulated Allis-Chalmers scraper retained with a 6418-9 elastic band. Two versions of the unpainted orange plastic scraper load were produced. The earliest Type I version had a windshield frame made of wire installed and had "ALLIS CHALMERS" heat-stamped in white on the scraper frame, and the raised "ALLIS CHALMERS" on the tractor hood picked out in black. The later Type II version lacked the wire windshield frame and had no colorful markings. The grille molding was modified as well. This version is much more abundant than the early version. The scraper was also available for separate sale through Lionel outlets, though packaged in a plain white box, or through Allis-Chalmers in a striped box. Also like the bulldozer, the scraper was fragile and is often found broken. The usual victims are the exhaust stack, the pin that couples the tractor to the scraper (this is often repaired with an insulating track pin), or again as with the bulldozer, the hydraulic cylinders

Unpainted flatcar. The prices shown below are predicated on the Type II scraper, if the Type I load is substituted, add a 30 percent premium. 350 450 600 6

Unpainted black flatcar 1250 2300 3500 8

6818 FLATCAR WITH TRANSFORMER: 1958 transformer heat-stamped "6818" on the upper panel, and "LIONEL TRANSFORMER CAR" was heat-stamped on the lower panel in white. 35 50 70 5

6819 Flatcar with Helicopter

6821 Flatcar with Crates

6822 Night Crew Searchlight

#	Description	VG	EX	LN	S
6819 FLATCAR WITH HELICOPTER: 1959-61, intended to be supplied with a non-operating helicopter, although occasionally they surface with an operating helicopter which was probably a substitution due to material shortages at Lionel. The non-operating helicopter had a gray fuselage and an opaque yellow tail rotor, it came both unmarked and heat-stamped "NAVY"		50	75	110	5
6820 AERIAL MISSILE TRANSPORT CAR: 1960-61, helicopter equipped with two huge, non-firing missiles		150	250	400	7
6821 FLATCAR WITH CRATES: 1959-60. Molded red flatcar with unmarked crate load retained by a 6418-9 elastic band		20	30	40	4
6822 NIGHT CREW SEARCHLIGHT: 1961-69. Superstructure gray plastic and searchlight housing black		25	40	60	4
Superstructure black plastic and searchlight housing gray		5	40	60	4
6823 FLATCAR WITH I.R.B.M. MISSILES: 1959-60 carried two 6650-type missiles. Each missile supported by 6801-64 boat cradle, and retained by 6418-9 silver elastic band. Both missiles in the pair matched and could be red over white, white over red or all-white		40	60	80	5

Handwritten notes in right margin: NO LOAN, REAR LOAN

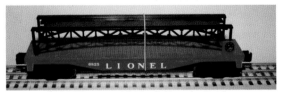

6825 Flatcar with Arch Trestle Bridge

6826 Flatcar with Christmas Trees

6827 P & H Power Shovel Car

#	Description	VG	EX	LN	S
6824 U.S.M.C. CABOOSE: 1960, cab, tool compartment, tool compartment insert and frame were all painted olive drab. The markings were all done in white: "U.S.M.C." The First-Aid Medical Car had a short black die-cast smokejack, a blue rubber figure with painted hands and face, a white plastic air tank and two white plastic stretchers with red cross markings .		125	200	300	7
6824 -50 FIRST AID CABOOSE: 1964, did not have crewman, tool compartment insert, stretchers or oxygen tank, frame was black with white heat-stamped sans-serif lettering.		50	100	150	7
6825 FLATCAR WITH ARCH TRESTLE BRIDGE: 1959-62, bridges can be found in both black and gray, although it is believed that only the black is the correct load for the flat car, although a car with the gray HO bridge makes a nice companion piece. Number was heat-stamped to the left of "LIONEL" . .		30	50	75	4
Number was heat-stamped to the right of "LIONEL".		30	50	75	4
6826 FLATCAR WITH CHRISTMAS TREES: 1959-60, with four spring-steel 2411-4 posts to keep the foliage load in place		100	150	215	5
6827 P & H POWER SHOVEL CAR: 1960-63, black flatcar was heat-stamped "6827" to the left of "LIONEL" in white. Its cargo was a well-detailed and elaborate kit of a P & H power shovel, which was packaged, along with the booklet "P & H: The Story of a Trademark," in a special yellow and black P & H box.		125	175	250	6

6830 Submarine Car

6844 Missile Carrying Car

6844 Missile Carrying Case

#	Description	VG	EX	LN	S
6828 P & H MOBILE CONSTRUCTION CRANE CAR: 1960-63, 1966, load was a kit of a crane produced by the Harnischfeger Corporation. This kit, in its own yellow and black P & H box, was packaged along with the flatcar inside a Lionel box.					
	Flatcar was unpainted black plastic.........	150	225	300	6
	Unpainted red plastic flatcar	500	650	850	8
6830 SUBMARINE CAR: 1960-61, with a non-operating Lionel submarine was produced with 6830 black heat-stamped number on sub	100	140	200	6
6844 MISSILE CARRYING CAR: 1959-60, rack held six white 44-40 missiles.					
	Unpainted black plastic frames............	45	70	110	5
	Unpainted red plastic frames	600	750	1200	8
UNNUMBERED FLATCAR: Gray unpainted 1877-style flatcar with no markings, no truss rods and AAR-type trucks. Carried either a moss-green tank or moss-Jeep and cannon, made by Payton Plastics................	There is not sufficient information to determine market value, however, an authentic load is key to its scarcity.			
UNMARKED HOPPER: 1963-69 short hopper.					
	Bright yellow	30	40	50	5
	Dark yellow	15	20	30	4
	Red body	30	45	60	5
	Black body	30	45	60	5
	Gray body	15	18	25	3
	Olive body	50	75	110	6

NO LOAD

020 90 Degree Crossover

022 Remote Control Switches

Lionel Accessories

Accessories are the second largest group of collectibles produced by Lionel during the postwar era. These items represented a large profit potential for the company, and were featured prominently in its advertising. Nevertheless, with very few exceptions all accessories are harder to find than the actual trains, and the scarcities shown are relative to other accessories, not Lionel production as a whole.

# Description	VG	EX	LN	S
011-11 INSULATING PINS: 1946-60, one dozen pieces.	1	2	3	2
011-43 INSULATING PINS: 1961, one dozen pieces..	1	2	3	2
020 90 DEGREE CROSSOVER: 1945- 1961. . . .	5	7	10	2
020X 45 DEGREE CROSSING: 1945-1959.	6	9	14	3
022 REMOTE CONTROL SWITCHES: 1945-66 pair, with controllers.	60	75	90	2
022LH REMOTE CONTROL SWITCH: 1950-61, left-hand 0 gauge turnout with controller. . . .	35	45	55	4
022RH REMOTE CONTROL SWITCH: 1950-61, right-hand 0 gauge turnout with controller.. . .	35	45	55	4

30 Water Tower

025 Bumper

30 Water Tower

#	Description	VG	EX	LN	S
022A REMOTE CONTROL SWITCH: 1947, without fixed voltage capabilities or bottom plates. Rather than the normal pair of 022C controllers, these switches were furnished with a single 1121C-60 control to operate the pair. The nameplates on these switches are stamped "022A".		100	150	275	8
022-500 0 GAUGE ADAPTER SET: 1957-61, allows the use of 0 gauge switches with Super 0 track.		2	3	4	4
025 BUMPER: 1946-47.		15	20	30	3
26 BUMPER: 1948-50.					
Die-cast housing painted gray.		30	40	50	6
Die-cast housing painted red.		10	15	25	4
30 WATER TOWER: 1947-50.					
Dark gray die-cast base, tank was translucent amber plastic lined with Kraft paper. Brown supports, gray roof with unplugged hole in center.		100	175	275	5
Black supports, gray roof with unplugged hole in center.		100	175	275	5
Black supports, brown roof with unplugged hole in center.		100	160	250	4
Late production with single-walled tank. Brown supports, revised gray roof did not have hole in the center.		80	125	200	3
31 CURVED TRACK: 1957-66, Super 0.		1	2	4	4

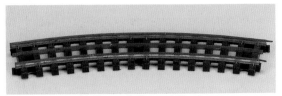

31 Super 0 Curved Track

32 Super 0 Straight Track

# Description	VG	EX	LN	S
31-7 POWER BLADE CONNECTOR: 1957-60, envelope contains 12 copper connectors.....	1	2	3	3
31-15 GROUND RAIL PIN: 1957-66, one dozen pins for outer rails of Super 0 track.	1	2	3	3
31-45 POWER BLADE CONNECTOR: 1961-64, envelope contains 12 copper connectors.....	1	2	3	3
32 STRAIGHT TRACK: 1957-66, Super 0	2	4	6	5
32-10 INSULATING PIN: 1957-60, one dozen insulating pins for use in the outer rails of Super 0 track..........................	1	2	3	4
32-20 POWER BLADE INSULATOR: 1957-60, this package contained one dozen insulating connectors for use on the center power blade of Super 0 track.......................	1	2	3	4
32-45 POWER BLADE INSULATOR: 1961-66, this package contained one dozen insulating connectors for use on the center power blade of Super 0 track.......................	1	2	3	4
32-55 INSULATING PIN: 1961-66, one dozen insulating pins for use in the outer rails of Super 0 track..........................	1	2	3	4

35 Boulevard
Lamp

38 Water Tower

#	Description	VG	EX	LN	S
33 HALF CURVED TRACK: 1957-66, half section of Super 0 curved track.................		1	2	3	5
34 HALF STRAIGHT TRACK: 1957-66, half section of Super 0 straight track...........		1	2	3	5
35 BOULEVARD LAMP: 1945-49............		20	35	55	5
36 OPERATING CAR REMOTE CONTROL SET: 1957-66, track set includes two control blades, a 90 controller and the needed hook-up wire. This allowed operating cars powered through sliding shoes to be operated on Super 0 track.		8	12	18	5
37 UNCOUPLING TRACK SET: 1957-66, 1 1/2-inch long Super 0 track section containing an electromagnet. Packaged with a 90 controller and hook-up wire.		10	15	20	5
38 WATER TOWER: 1946-47, with internal pump. Supplied with a turned metal finial to plug the roof top fill hole, a small funnel and a packet of tablets to use to color the water. Black supporting structure and either brown or dark gray-painted roof..................		275	375	500	7
Brown supporting structure and red roof.		250	325	450	6
38 ACCESSORY ADAPTER TRACKS: 1957-61, pair of special Super 0 tracks with only four crossties was needed to allow the attachment of track trips or installation on accessory bases.		8	12	15	4

40 Hook-Up
Wire

042 Manual
Switches

#	Description	VG	EX	LN	S
40 HOOK-UP WIRE: 1950-51, 1953-63, orange or gray reels, wrapped with 50 feet of 18-gauge single conductor wire insulated in either yellow, maroon, blue or white plastic. The earlier production was wrapped in Lionel imprinted cellophane..		5	20	40	5
40-25 CABLE REEL: 1955-57, orange reel holding 15 inches of the same black four-conductor wire as used on Lionel remote control track sections. It came packaged in a preprinted manila envelope, and it is that envelope that actually has the values listed here.		75	150	300	7
40-50 CABLE REEL: 1960-61, this orange reel holds 15 inches of the same black three-conductor wire as used on Lionel switch controls. It came packaged in a preprinted manila envelope, and it is that envelope that actually has the values listed here.		75	150	300	7
042 MANUAL SWITCHES: 1946-59, pair of manually operated 0 gauge turnouts.		40	50	60	4
43 POWER TRACK: 1959-66, special Super 0 1 1/2-inch track section with built-in fahnstock clips.		5	7	10	3
44-80 MISSILES: 1959-60, set of four replacement missiles.		10	20	30	7

45 Gateman

49 Insulated
Curved Track

64 Highway Lamp
Post

# Description	VG	EX	LN	S
45 GATEMAN: 1946-49.	40	50	60	2
45N GATEMAN: 1945.	50	65	80	5
48 INSULATED STRAIGHT TRACK: 1957-66, Super 0.	5	7	10	5
49 INSULATED CURVED TRACK: 1957-66, Super 0.	5	7	10	5
56 LAMP POST: 1946-49.	30	45	60	4
58 LAMP POST: 1946-50 Ivory-colored.	35	50	65	5
61 GROUND LOCK ON: 1957-66, Super 0.	1	2	3	5
62 POWER LOCK ON: 1957-66, Super 0.	1	2	3	5
64 HIGHWAY LAMP POST: 1945-49.	45	60	75	6
70 LAMP POST: 1949-50, has a die-cast tilting head.	25	40	60	4
71 LAMP POST: 1949-59.	15	20	30	3
75 GOOSE NECK LAMPS: 1961-63, pair of 6 1/2-inch tall black plastic lamps.	15	25	40	4

76 Boulevard
Street Lamps

89 Flagpole

92 Circuit Breaker
Controller, blister
pack

# Description	VG	EX	LN	S
76 BOULEVARD STREET LAMPS: 1956-69, green plastic.	15	25	40	3
88 CONTROLLER: 1946-50.	1	2	10	2
89 FLAGPOLE: 1956-58, stitched-edged flag.. . .	30	50	75	4
no stitch edge.	25	40	60	4
90 CONTROLLER: 1955-66.				
With shiny metal clip retaining a piece of cardstock.	3	8	14	3
No metal clip.	1	2	10	2
"No. 90 CONTROL" molded into the case.	1	2	10	2
91 CIRCUIT BREAKER: 1957-60.	20	25	30	6
92 CIRCUIT BREAKER CONTROLLER:				
Packaged in a manila envelope.	5	10	15	4
Packed in a traditional box.	5	10	15	4
Carded blister pack.	-	90	150	7
93 WATER TOWER: 1946-49, painted silver. . . .	25	40	65	4
96C CONTROLLER: 1945-54.	1	2	5	2
97 COAL ELEVATOR: 1946-50.	100	175	225	5

110 Trestle Set

111 Trestle Set

114 News Stand
with Horn

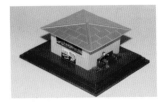

# Description	VG	EX	LN	S
108 TRESTLE SET: 1959, packaged in overstamped 1044 transformer box. Only 12 trestle piers provided (two each lettered A-F).	30	45	85	6
109 TRESTLE SET: 1961, set of 12 piers.	No value established.			8
110 TRESTLE SET: 1955-69.	18	22	35	2
111 TRESTLE SET: 1956-69 set of 10 "A" piers.. .	15	25	35	4
112 SUPER 0 SWITCHES: 1957 only, pair..	55	90	100	5
112R SUPER 0 SWITCHES: 1958-66 pair..	65	100	125	3
112-125 SUPER 0 SWITCH: 1957-61, left-hand remote control with 022C controller..	40	60	80	5
112-150 SUPER 0 SWITCH: 1957-61, right-hand remote control with 022C controller..	40	60	80	5
112LH SUPER 0 SWITCH: 1962-66, left hand remote control turnout with a 022C controller.	40	60	80	5
112RH SUPER 0 SWITCH: 1962-66, right hand remote control turnout with a 022C controller.	40	60	80	5
114 NEWS STAND WITH HORN: 1957-59. . . .	75	115	150	4

115 Lionel City Station

123 Lamp Assortment

123-60 Lamp Assortment

#	Description	VG	EX	LN	S
115 LIONEL CITY STATION: 1946-49.........		250	350	500	5
118 NEWSSTAND WITH WHISTLE: 1957-58..		60	100	125	4
119 LANDSCAPED TUNNEL: 1957-58 14 inches long, 10 inches wide, 8 inches high vacu-formed plastic tunnel..................		Too infrequently offered in Lionel packaging to establish value.			
120 90 DEGREE CROSSING: 1957-66, 90 degree Super 0 crossing.......................		5	10	15	4
121 LANDSCAPED TUNNEL: 1959-66, styrofoam tunnel. The Lionel packaging is essential to its value as a Lionel collectible...		Too infrequently offered in Lionel packaging to establish value.			
123 LAMP ASSORTMENT: 1953-59..........		150	250	400	7
123-60 LAMP ASSORTMENT: 1960-63.......		200	300	500	7
125 WHISTLE SHACK: 1950-55. Dark gray base.		25	45	60	4
Bright green base.		30	55	70	5
Dark green base..		30	55	70	5
Light gray base.		25	45	60	4
128 ANIMATED NEWSSTAND: 1957-60......		125	175	225	4
130 60 DEGREE CROSSING: 1957-66, Super 0 60 degree crossing......................		10	14	18	6

132 Illuminated Station with Automatic
Train Control

138 Water Tank

#	Description	VG	EX	LN	S
131 CURVED TUNNEL: 1957-66, styrofoam tunnel Lionel packaging is essential to its value as a Lionel collectible.	Too infrequently offered in Lionel packaging to establish value.			
132 ILLUMINATED STATION WITH AUTOMATIC TRAIN CONTROL: 1949-55, brick red chimney.	75	110	150	3
133 ILLUMINATED PASSENGER STATION: 1957, 1961-62, 1966, green chimney.	50	75	100	3
138 WATER TANK: 1953-57. Unpainted gray plastic roof.	125	175	200	5
Unpainted bright orange plastic roof.	100	150	175	3
140 AUTOMATIC BANJO SIGNAL: 1954-66. Packed in a box.	30	40	55	4
Blister packed to card.	-	150	250	7
142 MANUAL SWITCHES: 1957-66, pair Super 0 manual turnouts.	30	40	55	4
142-125 SUPER 0 SWITCH: 1957-61, single left-hand Super 0 manual.	20	30	40	5
142-150 SUPER 0 SWITCH: 1957-61, single right-hand Super 0 manual.	20	30	40	5

145 Automatic Gateman

150 Telegraph Pole Set

# Description	VG	EX	LN	S
142LH SUPER 0 SWITCH: 1962, separate sale left hand Super 0 manual turnout............	20	30	40	5
142RH SUPER 0 SWITCH: 1962, separate sale right hand Super 0 manual turnout........	20	30	40	5
145 AUTOMATIC GATEMAN: 1950-66........	30	40	55	2
145C CONTACTOR: 1950-60, SPST pressure-activated normally open momentary contact switch. Collectible value is in the box.......	1	2	10	1
147 WHISTLE CONTROLLER: 1961-66, contained a D cell battery...............	2	4	10	2
148 DWARF SIGNAL: 1957-60, furnished with 148C switch..........................	50	65	100	6
150 TELEGRAPH POLE SET: 1947-50, set of six brown plastic poles with metal base clips. ...	40	60	75	5

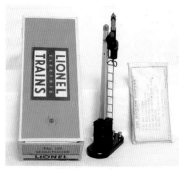

151 Semaphore

153 Automatic
Block Signal &
Control

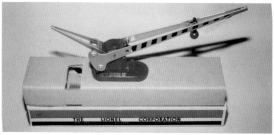

152 Automatic Crossing Gate

#	Description	VG	EX	LN	S
151 SEMAPHORE: 1947-69.					
	Green base, arrow on the semaphore arm raised, bulk of blade painted yellow.........	50	85	110	6
	Black base, arrow on the semaphore arm raised, bulk of blade painted yellow.........	20	28	40	3
	Black base, arrow on the semaphore arm raised, bulk of blade painted red.	80	125	200	7
	Arrow in the semaphore arm recessed, yellow arrow trim............................	20	28	40	3
	In carded blister pack.	-	190	300	7
152 AUTOMATIC CROSSING GATE: 1945-49,					
	main and pedestrian gates painted silver.....	20	40	55	5
153 AUTOMATIC BLOCK SIGNAL AND CONTROL: 1945-59...................		30	40	50	3
153C CONTACTOR: single pole, double throw pressure-activated momentary contact switch.					
	Collectible value is in box.	1	2	10	1
154 AUTOMATIC HIGHWAY SIGNAL: 1956-69.					
	Die-cast crossbuck painted white.	30	40	50	3
	Crossbuck molded white plastic with raised black lettering.........................	30	40	50	3
	In a carded blister pack.	-	150	250	7
155 BELL RINGING SIGNAL: 1955-57,					
	No "feet."	45	60	75	4
	Feet molded into the base................	45	60	75	4

156 Illuminated Station Platform

157 Illuminated Station Platform

# Description	VG	EX	LN	S
156 ILLUMINATED STATION PLATFORM: 1946-51, two sections of black plastic picket fence between roof supports, and provided with a separate fence section to connect two or more platforms together. Four lithographed tin miniature billboards hung from the fences. . .	60	85	125	4
157 ILLUMINATED STATION PLATFORM: 1952-59, four lithographed tin miniature billboards hung from fences.				
Red plastic base and dark green roof.	40	65	85	5
Maroon plastic base and medium green roof..	30	45	60	4
161 MAIL PICKUP SET: 1961-1963..	65	100	140	6
163 SINGLE TARGET BLOCK SIGNAL: 1961-69.Packaged in box.	30	40	55	3
Packed in blister packaging.	-	225	300	7
164 LOG LOADER: 1946-50, power terminals protruded through the top of the base, adjacent to the loading bin.	150	225	350	4
167 WHISTLE CONTROLLER: 1946-57.	4	8	15	1
175 ROCKET LAUNCHER: 1958-60.	125	250	400	6
175-50 EXTRA ROCKET: 1959-60. Replacement rockets for the 175 launcher and 6175 flatcar. Prices shown are for original six-pack box. . .	150	225	400	8

182 Triple Action Magnet Crane

193 Industrial Water Tower

# Description	VG	EX	LN	S
182 TRIPLE ACTION MAGNET CRANE: 1946-49, a nicely detailed electro-magnet, which lifted the 182-22 scrap steel supplied with the crane, was marked "Cutler Hammer."				
Note: The cab of the 182 ALWAYS had a smokestack, and the smokestack was NEVER molded as part of the cab.				
Clear-molded smokestack painted gray..	150	250	325	5
Smokestack painted black, matching the cab perfectly.	150	250	325	5
192 OPERATING CONTROL TOWER: 1959-60.	150	200	275	5
193 INDUSTRIAL WATER TOWER: 1953-55, with flashing red warning light.				
Supporting structure painted black.	100	150	200	7
Supporting structure painted red.	85	115	160	4
195 FLOODLIGHT TOWER: 1957-69.	45	60	75	3
195-75 EIGHT BULB FLOODLIGHT EXTENSION: 1957-60, this was a standard eight-bulb array from a 195 floodlight tower, plus two extension posts. This could be used to increase the light output from a 195.	20	35	60	5
196 SMOKE PELLETS: 1946-47, contained 100 smoke pellets made of ammonium nitrate for use in bulb-type smoke units only.	40	75	125	7

199 Microwave Relay Tower

206 Artificial
Coal

# Description	VG	EX	LN	S
197 ROTATING RADAR ANTENNA: 1957-59.				
Platform structure orange..............	100	125	190	5
Platform structure gray.	80	100	150	3
199 MICROWAVE RELAY TOWER: 1958-59...	40	75	120	5
206 ARTIFICIAL COAL: 1946-59, half-pound cloth bags lettered with red "No. 206" "ARTIFICIAL COAL" and Lionel markings, filled with ground Bakelite "coal."	5	10	15	3
214 PLATE GIRDER BRIDGE: 1953-69.				
Raised "LIONEL" lettering highlighted in white................................	15	20	30	3
Without white highlighting on the lettering..	15	20	30	3
"U. S. STEEL" cast into girders instead of "LIONEL".	20	25	40	3
"U. S. STEEL" and "6418" cast into girders...	20	25	40	3
Carded and blister packed..............	-	300	500	7
252 CROSSING GATE: 1950-63.............	25	30	40	2
253 AUTOMATIC BLOCK SIGNAL: 1956-59.				
Tan plastic base with simulated relay box portion painted black.	30	45	60	6
Entire plastic base left unpainted.........	20	30	45	4
256 FREIGHT STATION: 1950-53.				
Dark green roof......................	40	60	75	4
Lighter, brighter green roof..............	75	125	175	6

262 Highway Crossing Gate, blister pack

264 Operating Fork Lift

#	Description	VG	EX	LN	S
257 FREIGHT STATION WITH DIESEL HORN: 1956-57, the correct base has "257" molded into it.					
	Dark green roof and a maroon base..........	60	75	100	4
	Much lighter, brighter green roof molding. ..	75	125	175	6
	Dark green roof and brown base..........	80	100	120	4
260 BUMPER: 1951-69.					
	Red-painted die-cast metal...............	15	20	25	3
	Unpainted black plastic housing. Packaged in carded blisterpack. Most of the value indicated is for the intact packaging........	-	200	300	7
	Black plastic bumper packaged in a box.	30	40	50	5
262 HIGHWAY CROSSING GATE: 1962-69.					
	Packaged in box........................	50	75	100	4
	Packed in blister packaging. The value here solely is in the packaging...............	-	100	150	6
264 OPERATING FORK LIFT: 1957-60........	250	325	400	6
282 GANTRY CRANE: 1954-55, electromagnet has blackened sheet metal housing, crane cab screwed in place.......................	140	190	250	6
282R GANTRY CRANE: 1956-57. electromagnet housing bright metal, crane cab was snapped in place............................	140	190	250	6
299 CODE TRANSMITTER SET: 1961-63, packaged with a 299-25 telegraph key.......	100	125	175	6

308 Railroad Sign Set

309 Yard Sign Set

313 Bascule Bridge

#	Description	VG	EX	LN	S
308 RAILROAD SIGN SET: 1945-49, included five different die-cast sign posts..............		35	50	75	5
309 YARD SIGN SET: 1950-59, nine plastic signs with die-cast metal bases................		20	30	45	4
310 BILLBOARD: 1950-68, five unpainted green plastic billboard frames furnished with perforated die-cut sheets of cardboard billboards..........................		5	10	40	1
313 BASCULE BRIDGE: 1946-49, L-shaped gearbox. Supplied with a black steel alignment frame................................		300	525	675	5
313-82 FIBER PINS: 1946-60, one dozen 027 insulating pins.........................		1	2	3	2
313-121 FIBER PINS: 1961, one dozen 027 insulating pins.........................		1	2	3	2
314 PLATE GIRDER BRIDGE: 1945-50, gray rounded-end die-cast girder sides rubber-stamped "LIONEL" in black..............		25	35	50	3
315 ILLUMINATED TRESTLE BRIDGE: 1946-47, with red light mounted mid-span..........		75	100	125	5
316 TRESTLE BRIDGE: 1949................		25	40	55	4

321 Trestle Bridge

334 Dispatching Board

346 Operating Culvert Unloader

#	Description	VG	EX	LN	S
317 TRESTLE BRIDGE: 1950-56.............		25	35	50	3
321 TRESTLE BRIDGE: 1958-64, sheet metal base with unpainted gray plastic sides and top. It was shipped unassembled and the buyer was to assemble it..........................		20	35	50	3
332 ARCH UNDER BRIDGE: 1959-66, gray plastic sides with black-painted metal deck. It was shipped unassembled and the buyer was to assemble it..........................		30	45	60	4
334 DISPATCHING BOARD: 1957-60.........		175	250	310	5
342 CULVERT LOADER: 1956-58, came with 6342..........		200	275	350	5
345 CULVERT UNLOADING STATION: 1957-59, came with 6342.......................		250	350	425	6
346 OPERATING CULVERT UNLOADER: 1965-66, manual version of the 345.............		100	150	250	6
347 CANNON FIRING RANGE SET: 1964.....		200	600	1000	8
348 OPERATING CULVERT UNLOADER: 1966-69, manual version of the 345. Came with 6342..................................		125	175	250	6

350 Engine Transfer Table

350-50 Transfer Table Extension

352 Ice Depot

# Description	VG	EX	LN	S
350 ENGINE TRANSFER TABLE: 1957-60.....	150	325	450	5
350-50 TRANSFER TABLE EXTENSION: 1957-60.................	125	175	225	6
352 ICE DEPOT: 1955-57, came with 6352 ice car. Unpainted brown plastic platform, car with four lines of rubber-stamped data on the ice compartment door.....................	175	275	350	5
Unpainted red plastic platform, car with four lines of rubber-stamped data on the ice compartment door.	175	250	325	4
Unpainted red plastic platform, car with three lines of heat-stamped lettering on the door. . . .	225	315	400	6
353 TRACK SIDE CONTROL SIGNAL: 1960-61..............................	20	30	45	5
356 OPERATING FREIGHT STATION: 1952-57, dark green roof, with one each dark green and orange baggage carts. Came with a colorful lithographed tin insert for one of the baggage carts.................................	150	185	250	7
With dark green and orange baggage carts without the lithographed loads.	60	95	140	4
With one tomato red baggage cart and one light green baggage cart.	125	160	220	6
With light green colored roof.	90	125	175	5

362 Barrel Loader

362-78 Barrels

364 Lumber Loader

# Description	VG	EX	LN	S
362 BARREL LOADER: 1952-57.				
With white rubber man and red highlighted "LIONEL" sign.	150	200	275	7
With white rubber man and gold highlighted "LIONEL" sign.	90	125	175	5
With blue rubber man with painted face and hands, gold highlighted "LIONEL" sign.	70	100	150	4
Unpainted blue figure, gold highlighted "LIONEL" sign.	70	100	150	4
362-78 BARRELS: 1952-57, box of six brown-stained small wooden barrels.	5	10	20	3
364 LUMBER LOADER: 1948-57.				
Dark crackle gray finish.	100	150	200	5
Light gray hammer tone finish.	90	125	175	4
364C ON-OFF SWITCH: 1959-64.	2	8	16	5
365 DISPATCHING STATION: 1958-59.	80	115	140	4
375 TURNTABLE: 1962-64.	125	175	225	5
390C SWITCH: 1960-64.	5	10	20	7

394 Rotary Beacon

395 Floodlight Tower

# Description	VG	EX	LN	S
394 ROTARY BEACON: 1949-53, lightweight metal and plastic beacon housing embossed "LIONEL".				
Painted red.	30	40	55	3
Painted dark green.	50	75	100	5
Made of unpainted aluminum.	20	30	45	3
Red steel base with unpainted aluminum tower and platform.	30	40	55	4
395 FLOODLIGHT TOWER: 1949-56.				
Silver-painted steel structure..	25	40	60	3
Green-painted steel tower.	25	40	60	3
Made of unpainted aluminum.	30	45	70	4
Painted red	30	50	75	4
Painted yellow.	100	140	200	6
397 COAL LOADER: 1948-57.				
Large GM motor housing was painted yellow, and a number 70 Yard Light was screwed to the base.	250	350	450	7
No light, motor housing painted blue.	125	175	225	4
410 BILLBOARD BLINKER: 1956-58.	30	50	70	5
413 COUNTDOWN CONTROL PANEL: 1962 only.	45	75	100	5
415 DIESEL FUELING STATION: 1955-67.	100	145	200	5

419 Heliport

445 Operating Switch Tower

#	Description	VG	EX	LN	S
419 HELIPORT: 1962-only, included yellow helicopter..	175	425	600	6
443 MISSILE LAUNCHING PLATFORM WITH EXPLODING AMMUNITION DUMP: 1960-62.	25	40	80	4
445 OPERATING SWITCH TOWER: 1952-57. .	40	75	100	3
448 MISSILE FIRING RANGE SET: 1961-63, with 6448 Target Range Car with red sides and white lettering, roof and ends. Accessory packaged with lichen "bushes.".	90	175	250	5
450 SIGNAL BRIDGE: 1952-58, included two signal heads.	50	65	80	4
450L SIGNAL BRIDGE HEAD: 1952-58, blackened die-cast twin lamp socket. Much of the value is in the small Traditional box it was packed in..	40	60	100	6
452 GANTRY SIGNAL BRIDGE: 1961-63.	75	110	150	6

455 Operating Oil Derrick

456 Coal Ramp

#	Description	VG	EX	LN	S
455 OPERATING OIL DERRICK: 1950-54, furnished with four turned solid aluminum oil drums and a separate sign reading "SUNOCO OIL DERRICK No. 455".					
Dark green tower with a red platform near its top.	200	250	300	4
Dark green tower, with matching upper platform.	175	225	275	4
Pale green tower.	300	400	500	7
456 COAL RAMP: 1950-55, supplied with a special 456-100 controller, a 3456 operating hopper car, 456-83 maroon plastic receiving bin, two 456-85 coal pin mounting posts, a 456-84 coal bin door and a bag of 206 coal.					
Dark gray, braided steel wire handrails.	200	275	350	6
Dark gray, handrails made of fishing line.	175	250	325	6
Light gray, fishing line handrails.	150	225	300	5
460 PIGGY BACK TRANSPORTATION SET: 1955-57, came with 3460 flatcar and trailers. With two green plastic "LIONEL TRAINS" trailers with "FRUEHAUF" and "DURAVAN" signs on the front. Self-adhesive sign on forklift reads "ROSS TRAILOADER".	100	150	175	4
"ROSS TRAILOADER" markings rubber-stamped in white.	125	175	200	5
460P PIGGY BACK PLATFORM: Platform only without trailers or flatcar. The box must be present in order for this to have any real value.	300	500	700	6

461 Platform with Truck & Trailer

464 Lumber Mill

#	Description	VG	EX	LN	S
461 PLATFORM WITH TRUCK AND TRAILER: 1966, lacks depressions molded into the top to receive trailer wheels. Came with a white single axle Lionel-made trailer and a red die-cast tractor made by Midge...............		100	150	200	6
462 DERRICK PLATFORM SET: 1961-62, with two 6805-type containers without illumination but with wire bales attached to handles......		200	275	350	6
464 LUMBER MILL: 1956-60...............		125	175	225	4
465 SOUND DISPATCHING STATION: 1956-57, came with a gray plastic microphone equipped with two red buttons.		100	140	175	4
470 MISSILE LAUNCHING PLATFORM WITH EXPLODING TARGET CAR: 1959-62 came with exploding 6470 target car.		100	150	210	3
494 ROTARY BEACON: 1954-66.					
Red-painted steel.		30	40	50	3
Silver-painted steel		130	40	50	3
Unpainted aluminum.		30	40	50	3
497 COALING STATION: 1953-58.					
Dark green unpainted plastic roof..........		150	175	250	5
Light green unpainted plastic roof.........		125	160	230	4
671-75 SPECIAL SMOKE BULB:		10	20	30	5

760 072 Track

902 Elevated Trestle Set

# Description	VG	EX	LN	S
703-10 SPECIAL SMOKE BULB:	15	30	45	6
760 072 TRACK: 1950, 1954-58, box of 16 sections of 072 track.	50	75	120	5
902 ELEVATED TRESTLE SET: 1959-60, came packaged in a paper sack printed with the label "902 ELEVATED TRESTLE SET".	-	100	250	8
908 RAILROAD TERMINAL: Circa 1964.	-	-	-	8
909 SMOKE FLUID: 1957-68.	5	20	45	4
910 U. S. NAVY SUBMARINE BASE: 1961, made entirely of cardboard.	-	-	-	8
919 ARTIFICIAL GRASS: 1946-64, half-pound bag of green-dyed sawdust.	7	7	25	2
920 SCENIC DISPLAY SET: 1957-58.	40	100	150	6
920-2 TUNNEL PORTALS: 1958-59, set of two "HILLSIDE" gray plastic tunnel portals.. . . .	20	35	50	5
920-3 GREEN GRASS: 1957-58, the clear plastic bag of green-dyed sawdust "grass.".	2	10	30	6

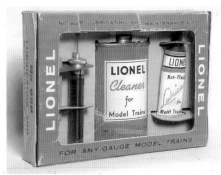

928 Maintenance & Lubricant Kit

943 Exploding Ammunition Dump

# Description	VG	EX	LN	S
920-4 YELLOW GRASS: 1957-58, the clear plastic bag of yellow-dyed sawdust "grass.". . .	2	10	30	6
920-5 ARTIFICIAL ROCK: 1957-1958, expanded vermiculite..	5	30	50	7
920-8 LICHEN: 1958.	5	25	50	7
927 LUBRICATING AND MAINTENANCE KIT: 1950-59..	10	30	60	3
928 MAINTENANCE AND LUBRICANT KIT: 1960-63	20	40	70	5
943 EXPLODING AMMUNITION DUMP: 1959-61.	30	60	90	4
950 U.S. RAILROAD MAP: 1958-66, packed in a tube.	60	90	150	4
951 FARM SET: 1958.	125	175	400	7
952 FIGURE SET: 1958.	125	175	400	7
953 FIGURE SET: 1959-62..	125	175	400	7
954 SWIMMING POOL AND PLAYGROUND SET: 1959.	125	175	400	7

957 Farm Building & Animal Set

960 Barnyard Set

# Description	VG	EX	LN	S
955 HIGHWAY SET: 1958.	125	175	400	7
956 STOCKYARD SET: 1959.	125	175	400	7
957 FARM BUILDING AND ANIMAL SET: 1958.	125	175	400	7
958 VEHICLE SET: 1958..	150	250	475	7
959 BARN SET: 1958.	150	250	475	7
960 BARNYARD SET: 1959-61.	125	175	400	7
961 SCHOOL SET: 1959.	125	175	400	7
962 TURNPIKE SET: 1958.	175	275	500	8
963 FRONTIER SET: 1959-60.	150	250	475	7
963-100 FRONTIER SET: 1960.	300	450	700	7
964 FACTORY SITE SET: 1959.	150	250	475	7
965 FARM SET: 1959.	125	175	400	7
966 FIRE HOUSE SET: 1958.	125	175	400	7

968 TV Transmitter Set

971 Lichen

# Description	VG	EX	LN	S
967 POST OFFICE SET: 1958.	125	175	400	7
968 TV TRANSMITTER SET: 1958.	150	250	475	7
969 CONSTRUCTION SET: 1960.	150	250	475	7
970 TICKET BOOTH: 1958–60, 46 inches tall, 22 inches wide, 11 inches deep cardboard ticket booth.	-	125	175	6
971 LICHEN: 1960-64.	75	175	300	8
972 LANDSCAPE TREE ASSORTMENT: 1961-64.	150	300	500	8
973 COMPLETE LANDSCAPING SET: 1960-64.	300	1000	1500	7
974 SCENERY SET: 1962-63.	700	2500	4000	8
980 RANCH SET: 1960.	125	200	400	7
981 FREIGHT YARD SET: 1960.	125	200	400	7
982 SUBURBAN SPLIT LEVEL SET: 1960.	125	200	400	7
983 FARM SET: 1960-61.	125	200	400	7

985 Freight Area Set

986 Farm Set

#	Description	VG	EX	LN	S
984 RAILROAD SET: 1961-62.	125	200	400	7
985 FREIGHT AREA SET: 1961.	125	200	400	7
986 FARM SET: 1962.	125	200	400	7
987 TOWN SET: 1962.	400	700	1000	8
988 RAILROAD STRUCTURE SET: 1962.	.150	275	450	8
1008 UNCOUPLING UNIT: 1957-62.	1	2	5	1
1008-50 UNCOUPLING TRACK SECTION: 1957-62..	1	2	5	1
1009 MANUMATIC UNCOUPLER:	1	2	5	1
1010 TRANSFORMER: 1961-66, 35-Watt.	10	20	25	2
1011 TRANSFORMER: 1948-52, 25-Watt.	10	15	20	2
1011X TRANSFORMER: 1948-52, 25-Watt, 125-volt, 25-cycle.	10	15	20	2
1012 TRANSFORMER: 1950-54, 35-Watt.	20	30	40	5

1020 90 Degree Crossing, blister packed

# Description	VG	EX	LN	S
1014 TRANSFORMER: 1955, 40-Watt.	15	25	40	2
1015 TRANSFORMER: 1955-60, 45-Watt..	25	35	45	2
1016 TRANSFORMER: 1959-60, 35-Watt, 110-Volt primary transformer had a speed control and circuit breaker, but no fixed voltage taps or whistle control.	10	20	30	2
1019 REMOTE CONTROL TRACK SET: 1946-50, 027 uncoupling track.	5	8	10	3
1020 90 DEGREE CROSSING: 1955-69, 027 90 degree crossing. Boxed..	2	4	7	3
Blister packed.	–	200	265	7
1021 90 DEGREE CROSSING: 1945-54, 027 90 degree crossing.	2	4	8	3
1022 MANUAL SWITCHES: 1953-69, pair of 027 turnouts..	15	20	30	3
1022LH MANUAL SWITCH: 1953-69, manual 027 left hand turnout. Conventional packaging.	8	10	16	3
Carded blister pack..	40	50	65	7

1023 45 Degree Crossing, blister packed

1033 Transformer

# Description	VG	EX	LN	S
1022RH MANUAL SWITCH: 1953-69, manual 027 right hand turnout.				
Conventional packaging.	8	10	16	3
Carded blister pack.	40	50	65	7
1023 45 DEGREE CROSSING: 1956-69, 027 crossing. Boxed.	3	6	10	3
Blister packed	-	260	375	7
1024 MANUAL SWITCHES: 1946-52, pair of 027 manual turnouts.	10	20	25	3
1025 ILLUMINATED BUMPER: 1946-47, die-cast black illuminated bumper, attached to a section of 027 straight track.	10	15	20	4
1025 TRANSFORMER: 1961-66, 1969, 45 watt.	25	35	45	2
1026 TRANSFORMER: 1961-64, 25 watt.	10	15	20	2
1032 TRANSFORMER: 1948, 75 watt.	20	35	60	3
1032M TRANSFORMER: 1948, 75 watt, 125 volt, 50 cycle.	30	45	70	7
1033 TRANSFORMER: 1948-56.	40	60	90	2
1034 TRANSFORMER: 1948-54, 75 watt.	20	35	60	3

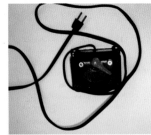

1043 Transformer

1043-500
Transformer

1047 Operating
Switchman

#	Description	VG	EX	LN	S
1035 TRANSFORMER: 1947, 60 watt.		5	10	15	1
1037 TRANSFORMER: 1946-47, 40 watt.		10	15	25	3
1041 TRANSFORMER: 1945-46, 60 watt.		20	35	50	4
1042 TRANSFORMER: 1947-48, 75 watt.		25	40	60	4
1043 TRANSFORMER: 1953-58, 50 watt.		20	35	50	3
1043-500 TRANSFORMER: Ivory-colored case, white cord and gold-colored handle, 60 watts.		75	125	175	6
1043M TRANSFORMER: 1953-58, 50 watt 125 volt, 25 cycle.		40	55	75	7
1044 TRANSFORMER: 1957-69, 90 watt.		40	65	90	3
1044M TRANSFORMER: 1957-69, 90 watt, 125 volt, 25 cycle.		40	65	90	7
1045 OPERATING WATCHMAN: 1946-50.		20	35	50	4
1047 OPERATING SWITCHMAN: 1959-61. . . .		90	125	170	6
1053 TRANSFORMER: 1956-60, 60 watt.		20	35	45	3

1122 Remote Control Switches

1122LH Switch, blister packed

# Description	VG	EX	LN	S
1063 TRANSFORMER: 1960-64, 75 watt.	25	40	60	3
1063-100 TRANSFORMER: 1961, 75 watt.	30	45	65	5
1073 TRANSFORMER: 1961-66, 60 Watt.	20	30	50	3
1121 REMOTE CONTROL SWITCHES: 1946-51, pair of 027 turnouts.	20	35	45	3
1122 REMOTE CONTROL SWITCHES: 1952-53, pair of 027 turnouts.	17	30	35	4
1122E REMOTE CONTROL SWITCHES: 1953-69, pair of 027 turnouts.	20	35	45	3
1122LH SWITCH: 1955-69, single left-hand 027 turnout.	12	18	25	4
1122RH SWITCH: 1955-69, single right-hand 027 turnout.	12	18	25	4
1122-234 FIBER PINS: 1958-60, one dozen 027 insulating pins.	1	2	3	2
1122-500 0-27 GAUGE ADAPTER: 1957-66, conversion pins to use 027 switches with Super 0 track.	1	2	3	3

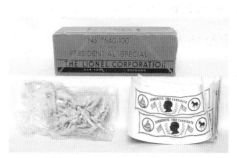

1640-100 Presidential Special

3330-100 Operating Submarine Kit

# Description	VG	EX	LN	S
1144 TRANSFORMER: 1961-66, 75 watt.	10	20	40	3
1232 TRANSFORMER: 1948, 75 watt, 220 volt primary.	50	100	150	7
1241 TRANSFORMER: 1947-48, 60 watt, 220 volt primary.	50	100	150	7
1244 TRANSFORMER: 1957-66, 90 watt, 220 volt primary.	50	100	150	5
1640-100 PRESIDENTIAL SPECIAL: 1960. Bag of plastic people and paper signs for passenger cars indicating Secret Service, Press Corps and both political parties.	100	225	400	7
3330-100 OPERATING SUBMARINE KIT: 1960-61, packaged in cardboard box with elaborate artwork.	100	200	300	5
6009 UNCOUPLING SECTION: 1953-55, 027. . .	3	6	10	3
6019 REMOTE CONTROL TRACK: 1948-66, 027.	4	6	10	2
6029 UNCOUPLING TRACK SET: 1955-63, 027.	3	5	7	2
6149 REMOTE CONTROL UNCOUPLING TRACK: 1964-69, 027.	1	5	7	1

ECU-1 Electronic Control Unit

KW Transformer

# Description	VG	EX	LN	S
6418 BRIDGE: See 214.				
6800-60 AIRPLANE: 1957-58, individually boxed for separate sale.	150	350	450	6
A TRANSFORMER: 1947-48, 90 watt.	20	40	50	3
A220 TRANSFORMER: 1947-48, 90 watt, 220 volt.	50	70	100	7
AX TRANSFORMER: 1947-48, 90 watt, 110 volt, 25 hertz primary.	20	40	50	6
CTC LOCKON: 1947-69.	-	-	1	1
ECU-1 ELECTRONIC CONTROL UNIT: 1946-49.	40	75	100	6
KW TRANSFORMER: 1950-65, 190 watts.	100	150	200	4
LTC LOCKON: 1950-69, illuminated.	2	5	12	3
LW TRANSFORMER: 1955-56, 125 watts.	75	100	125	4
OC CURVED TRACK: 1945-61, 0 gauge curved track.	-	.50	1	1

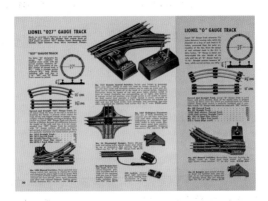

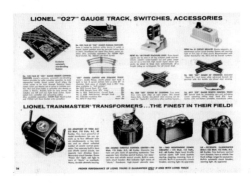

# Description	VG	EX	LN	S
OC-18 STEEL PINS: 1946-60, one dozen steel pins for 0 gauge track. The collectible is the envelope, not the pins.	-	-	1	3
OC-51 STEEL PINS: This small envelope, available only in 1961, contained one dozen steel pins for 0 gauge track. The collectible is the envelope, not the pins.	-	-	1	5
OS STRAIGHT TRACK: 1945-61, 0 gauge straight track.	.50	1	2	1
OTC LOCKON:	1	2	4	3
Q TRANSFORMER: 1946, 75 watts	20	40	60	6
R TRANSFORMER 1946, 100 watts, 1947, 110 watts.	50	75	100	6
RCS REMOTE CONTROL TRACK: 1946-48, 0 Gauge.	5	10	15	3
R220 TRANSFORMER: 1948, this transformer was the same as an R, but was adapted for the European market by the use of a 220-volt primary coil rather than the standard 110-volt US-type coil.	50	100	150	7
RW TRANSFORMER: 1948-54, 110 watts.	50	75	100	4

SW Transformer

TW Transformer

# Description	VG	EX	LN	S
S TRANSFORMER: 1947, 80 watts............	20	35	60	5
SW TRANSFORMER: 1961-66, 130 watts......	60	90	125	4
SP SMOKE PELLETS: 1948-69, bottle of 50 pills.	10	20	30	2
TOC CURVED TRACK: 1962-69, 0 gauge curved track.	-	.50	1	1
TOC-51 STEEL PINS: 1962-69, one dozen steel pins for 0 gauge track. The collectible is the envelope, not the pins.	-	-	1	3
TOS STRAIGHT TRACK: 1962-69, 0 gauge straight track.	50	1	2	1
TW TRANSFORMER: 1953-60, 175 watts......	75	125	150	4
T020 90 DEGREE CROSSOVER: 1962-69, 90 degree 0 gauge crossing.	5	7	10	2
T022-500 0 GAUGE ADAPTER SET: 1962-66, allows the use of 0 gauge switches with Super 0 track. Much of the value is in the packaging.	2	3	4	4
UCS REMOTE CONTROL TRACK: 1949-69, 0 gauge.	8	14	18	2

UTC Lockon

V Transformer

ZW Transformer

#	Description	VG	EX	LN	S
UTC LOCKON: 1945-46 fits Standard Gauge track as well as 0-27, and 0 gauge track..........		1	2	4	3
V TRANSFORMER: 1946-47, four-throttle 150 watts...............................		100	125	150	4
VW TRANSFORMER: 1948-49, four-throttle 150 watts...............................		120	140	175	5
Z TRANSFORMER: 1945-47, four-throttle 250 watts...............................		100	125	150	4
ZW TRANSFORMER: 1948-49, 250 watts......		100	150	250	4
1950-56, 275 watts...................		150	225	300	3
1957-66 ZW(R), although the "R" did not appear on the nameplate...............		150	225	300	3

Lionel Cataloged Outfits 1945-1969

While many of us think we got Lionel Train sets during the postwar period, a quick look at the period catalogs or boxes will reveal that in most cases we actually received Lionel outfits. Regardless of the terminology, today these outfits, when still with the original individual item boxes and the original outfit carton, are prized collector's items.

The same components, without the outer outfit carton, are just a group of trains and lose their outfit, or set, distinction, and much of the value listed here. In addition to the locomotives and rolling stock shown in these listings, outfits typically came with instruction books and sheets, wire, lock-on, accessory catalogs, brochures, smoke pellets and tampers (if applicable), and miniature billboards. All of these items must be present to realize the full value. Traditionally, 0-gauge and Super 0 outfits did not include a transformer, which was sold separately, while 027 outfits included a transformer. This situation changed in 1964, when a transformer was supplied with Super 0 outfit 13150. From that point on, transformers began to be supplied with more 0 and Super 0 outfits. One item, which normally can be missing from outfits today without affecting the value, is standard 027 or 0-gauge track. Unlike Super-0 track, 0 and 027 track is so common it is almost worthless, and most collectors feel that the damage caused to the boxes by the track rubbing on it exceeds the value of the track.

Because the value of an outfit is so dependent on the presence and condition of the outfit and component boxes, values are on listed for excellent and like new examples. The outfit number, year, catalog name, and the catalog numbers of major components, beginning with locomotive, are shown here.

Please note, Lionel produced many uncataloged outfits as well. Some were offered through the normal dealer network, others through mass merchandisers such as Sears and J.C. Penney, and others were used as premiums by firms such as Wix and Swift. These uncataloged outfits, some quite collectible, are not listed here. A final note, a "W" suffix on an outfit number indicated that the train whistled or had an operating horn; a "B" indicated an operating bell, "S" indicated the locomotive smoked.

463W 0-Gauge Four car freight set — Lionel's First
Postwar World II train set

#	Description	EX	LN	S
463W: 1945 0 Gauge Four-Car Freight Set: 224, 2466W, 2458, 2452, 2555, 2457	650	1200	8
1000W: 1955 027 Three-Car Set: 2016, 6026W, 6014 red, 6012, 6017	200	350	4
1001: 1955 027 Three-Car Set: 610, 6012, 6014 red, 6017	250	475	4
1111: 1948 Lionel Scout Set: 1001, 1001T, 1002 blue, 1005, 1007	125	225	2
1112: 1948 Lionel Scout Set: 1101, 1001T, 1002 blue, 1004, 1005, 1007	200	325	5
1113: 1950 Lionel Scout Train: 1120, 1001T, 1002 black, 1005, 1007	125	225	4
1115: 1949 Lionel Scout: 1110, 1001T, 1002 black, 1005, 1007	150	250	4
1117: 1949 Lionel Scout: 1110, 1001T, 1002 black, 1005, 1004, 1007	150	250	4
1119: 1951-52 Scout Three-Car Freight: 1110, 1001T, 1002 black, 1004, 1007.	125	225	3

1405 Freight Train Set

#	Description	EX	LN	S
1400: 1946 Lionel 027 Passenger Set: 221, 221T, two blue 2430 Pullmans, blue 2431 Observation . . .		650	1150	6
1400W: 1946 Lionel 027 Passenger Set: 221, 221W, two blue 2430 Pullmans, blue 2431 Observation.		750	1300	7
1401: 1946 Lionel 027 Freight Outfit: 1654, 1654T, 2452X, 2465, 2472		150	250	4
1401W: 1946 Lionel 027 Freight Outfit: 1654, 1654W, 2452X, 2465, 2472		250	450	7
1402: 1946 Lionel 027 Passenger Set: 1666, 2466T, two green 2440s, green 2441		500	750	6
1402W: 1946 Lionel 027 Passenger Set: 1666, 2466W, two green 2440s, green 2441		600	900	6
1403: 1946 Lionel 027 Freight Train: 221, 221T, 2411, 2465, 2472		425	650	5
1403W: 1946 Lionel 027 Freight Train: 221, 221W, 2411, 2465, 2472		525	775	6
1405: 1946 Lionel 027 Freight Train: 1666, 2466T, 2452X, 2465, 2472		175	300	4
1405W: 1946 Lionel 027 Freight Train: 1666, 2466W, 2452X, 2465, 2472		225	400	7

1946 Catalog

#	Description	EX	LN	S
1407B: 1946 Lionel 027 Switcher Bell Outfit: 1665, 2403B, 2452X, 2560, 2419	900	1500	7
1409: 1946 Lionel 027 Freight Train: 1666, 2466T, 3559, 2465, 3454, 2472	400	550	5
1409W: 1946 Lionel 027 Freight Train: 1666, 2466W, 3559, 2465, 3454, 2472	450	650	6
1411W: 1946 Freight Outfit: 1666, 2466WX, 2452X, 2465, 2454, 2472	225	375	5
1413WS: 1946 Lionel 027 Freight Train: 2020, 2020W, 2452X, 2465, 2454, 2472	350	525	4
1415WS: 1946 Lionel 027 Freight Set: 2020, 2020W, 3459, 3454, 2465, 2472	525	800	5
1417WS: 1946 Lionel 027 Freight Outfit: 2020, 2020W, 2465, 3451, 2560, 2419	750	1100	6
1419WS: 1946 Lionel 027 Freight Train: 2020, 2020W, 3459, 97, 2452X, 2560, 2419	900	1300	7
1421WS: 1946 Lionel 027 Freight Train: 2020, 2020W, 3451, 164, 2465, 3454, 2472	1000	1450	7

1426WS Passenger Set

#	Description	EX	LN	S
1423W: 1948 Lionel Three-Car outfit: 1655, 6654W, 6452, 6465, 6257		150	225	3
1949 Lionel Three-Car outfit: 1655, 6654W, 6462, 6465, 6257		150	225	3
1425B: 1948 Switcher Freight: 1656, 6403B, 6456 black, 6465, 6257X.		850	1250	6
1949 Switcher Freight: 1656, 6403B, 6456 black, 6465, 6257		850	1250	6
1426WS: 1948-49 Lionel Passenger Set: 2026, 6466WX, two green 2440 Pullmans, green 2441 Observation		600	1000	5
1427WS: 1948 Lionel Three-Car Freight Set: 2026, 6466WX, 6465, 6454, 6257		250	450	3
1429WS: 1948 Four-Car Freight Set: 2026, 6466WX, 3451, 6465, 6454, 6357		200	325	3
1430WS: 1948-49 Passenger Train: 2025, 6466WX, 2400, 2402, 2401		800	1500	5
1431: 1947 Lionel Freight Train: 1654, 1654T, 2452X, 2465, 2472.		150	250	5
1431W: 1947 Lionel Freight Train: 1654, 1654W, 2452X, 2465, 2472.		175	275	5

1435WS Freight Set with 2257 caboose
substituted for 2472

#	Description	EX	LN	S
1432: 1947 Lionel Passenger Set: 221, 221T, two blue 2430 Pullmans, blue 2431 Observation . . .		900	1500	5
1432W: 1947 Lionel Passenger Set: 221, 221W, two blue 2430 Pullmans, blue 2431 Observation . . .		900	1500	5
1433: 1947 Lionel Freight Train: 221, 221T, 2411, 2465, 2472		400	700	5
1433W: 1947 Lionel Freight Train: 221, 221W, 2411, 2465, 2472		400	725	5
1434WS: 1947 Passenger Train: 2025, 2466WX, two green 2440 Pullmans, green 2441 Observation.		400	725	5
1435WS: 1947 Lionel Freight Train: 2025, 2466WX, 2452X, 2454, 2472		250	375	3
1437WS: 1947 Lionel Freight Set: 2025, 2466WX, 2452X, 2465, 2454, 2472		275	450	4
1439WS: 1947 Lionel Freight Outfit: 2025, 2466WX, 3559, 2465, 3454, 2472		425	750	5
1441WS: 1947 De Luxe Work Outfit: 2020, 2020W, 2461, 3451, 2560, 2419		550	900	6
1443WS: 1947 Four-Car Freight: 2020, 2020W, 3459, 3462, 2465, 2472		425	750	5

1451WS Freight Set

#	Description	EX	LN	S
1445WS: 1948 Four-Car Freight: 2025, 6466WX, 3559, 6465, 6454, 6357		325	550	5
1447WS: De Luxe Work Train: 1948 2020, 6020W, 3451, 2461, 2460, 6419		525	950	5
1949 2020, 6020W, 3461, 6461, 2460, 6419		500	900	5
1449WS: 1948 Five-Car Freight Outfit: 2020, 6020W, 3462, 6465, 3459, 6411, 6357		450	800	5
1451WS: 1949 Three-Car Freight: 2026, 6466WX, 6462, 3464, 6257		275	450	4
1453WS: 1949 Four-Car Freight: 2026, 6466WX, 3464, 6465, 3461, 6357		325	525	4
1455WS: 1949 Four-Car 027 Freight: 2025, 6466WX, 6462, 6465, 3472, 6357		400	750	4
1457B:1949-50 Four-Car Diesel Freight: 6220, 6462, 3464, 6520, 6419		625	950	5
1459WS: 1949 027 Five-Car Freight Outfit: 2020, 6020W, 6411, 3656, 6465, 3469, 6357		550	900	5
1461S: 1950 Three-Car Freight With Smoke: 6110, 6001T, 6002, 6004, 6007		150	250	2

1464W Diesel Three-Car Set, 1950

1464W Diesel Three-Car Set, 1951

#	Description	EX	LN	S
1463W: 1950 027 Three-Car Freight: 2036, 6466W, 6462, 6465, 6257	150	250	2
1463WS: 1951 027 Three-Car Freight: 2026, 6466W, 6462, 6465, 6257	200	325	3
1464W: 1950 027 Diesel Three-Car Pullman: 2023 yellow A-A, 2481, 2482, 2483	2000	4000	6
1951 027 Diesel Three-Car Pullman: 2023 silver A-A, 2421, 2422, 2423 all with gray roofs	900	1500	4
1952-53 Three-Car Pullman: 2033 silver A-A, 2421, 2422, 2423 all with silver roofs	850	1400	3
1465: 1952 Three-Car Freight: 2034, 6066T, 6032, 6035, 6037	150	250	2
1467W: 1950 027 Diesel Four-Car Freight: 2023 yellow A-A, 6656, 6465, 6456, 6357	600	900	4
1951 2023 AA silver, 6656, 6465, 6456, 6357 . .	575	875	4
1952-53 Four-Car Freight: 2032 A-A, 6656, 6456, 6465, 6357	525	800	4
1469WS: 1950 027 Four-Car Freight: 2035, 6466W, 6462, 6465, 6456 black, 6257	225	425	3
1951 027 Four-Car Freight: 2035, 6466W, 6462, 6465, 6456 maroon, 6257	225	425	3
1471WS: 1950-51 Five-Car Freight: 2035, 6466W, 3469X, 6465, 6454, 3461X, 6357	350	575	3

1479WS Diesel Four-Car Freight Set

#	Description	EX	LN	S
1473WS: 1950 Four-Car Freight: 2046, 2046W, 3464, 6465, 6520, 6357	425	750	3
1475WS: 1950 Five-Car Freight: 2046, 2046W, 3656, 3461X, 6472, 3469X, 6419	575	975	6
1477S: 1951-52 027 Three-Car Freight: 2026, 6466T, 6012, 6014 white, 6017	200	375	3
1479WS: 1952 027 Four-Car Freight: 2056, 2046W, 6462, 6465, 6456, 6257	425	700	3
1481WS: 1951 Five-Car Freight: 2035, 6466W, 3464, 6465, 3472, 6462, 6357	325	525	3
1483WS: 1952 Five-Car Freight: 2056, 2046W, 3472, 6462, 3474, 6465, 6357	625	950	5
1484WS: Four-Car Pullman: 2056, 2046W, 2421, 2422, 2429, 2423 with silver roofs	950	1500	6
1485WS: 027 Three-Car Freight: 2025, 6466W, 6462, 6465, 6257	225	350	4
1500: 1953-54 027 Three-Car Freight: 1130, 6066T, 6032, 6034, 6037	100	150	1
1501S: 1953 027 Three-Car Freight: 2026, 6066T, 6032, 6035, 6037	125	200	2

1502WS Diesel Three-Car Pullman Set

#	Description	EX	LN	S
1502WS: 1953 027 Three-Car Pullman: 2055, 2046W, 2421, 2422, 2423		675	1100	5
1503WS: 1953 027 Four-Car Freight: 2055, 6026W, 6462 black, 6456 black, 6465, 6257		300	500	2
1954 027 Four-Car Freight: 2055, 6026W, 6462 green, 6456 maroon, 6465, 6257		300	500	2
1505WS: 1953 027 Four-Car Freight: 2046, 2046W, 6464-1, 6462, 6415, 6357.................		400	850	4
1507WS: 1953 027 Five-Car Freight: 2046, 2046W, 3472, 6415, 6462, 6468, 6357..............		425	900	4
1509WS: 1953 027 Five-Car Freight: 2046, 2046W, 3520, 6456, 3469, 6460, 6419..............		450	800	3
1511S: 1953 027 Four-Car Freight: 2037, 6066T, 6032, 3474, 6035, 6037		300	500	4
1513S: 1954-55 027 Four-Car Freight: 2037, 6026T, 6012, 6014 red, 6015, 6017		175	300	1
1515WS: 1954 027 Five-Car Freight: 2065, 2046W, 6415, 6462, 6464-25, 6456, 6357............		450	750	4
1516WS: 1954 027 Three-Car Passenger: 2065, 2046W, 2434, 2432, 2436		700	1125	5

1517W Diesel Four-Car Freight Set

1517W Diesel Four-Car Freight Set Boxed

# Description	EX	LN	S
1517W: 1954 027 Four-Car Freight: 2245P/C A-B, 6464-225, 6561, 6462 green, 6427	1000	1550	6
1519WS: 1954 027 Five-Car Freight: 2065, 6026W, 3461, 6462 red, 6356, 3482, 6427	550	975	5
1520W: 1954 027 Texas Special Three-Car Passenger: 2245P/C A-B, 2432, 2435, 2436 . . .	1800	2700	7
1521WS: 1954 027 Five-Car Freight: 2065, 2046W, 3620, 3562 black, 6561, 6460 black cA-B, 6419	750	1200	5
1523: 1954 027 Four-Car Work Train: 6250, 6511, 6456 gray, 6460 red cab, 6419	750	1200	5
1527: 1955 027 Three-Car Work Train: 1615, 1615T, 6462, 6560 gray cab, 6119	400	750	5
1529: 1955 027 Three-Car Freight: 2028, 6311, 6436, 6257	675	1000	6
1531W: 1955 027 Four-Car Freight: 2328, 6462 red, 6456, 6465, 6257	575	975	6
1533WS: 1955 027 Freight Hauler: 2055, 6026W, 3562 yellow, 6436, 6465, 6357	425	725	5
1534W: 1955 027 Three-Car Passenger: 2328, 2434, 2432, 2436	950	1500	6

1541WS Five-Car Freight Set

1541WS Five-Car Freight Set Boxed

#	Description	EX	LN	S
1536W: 1955 027 Three-Car Passenger: 2245P/C A-B, 2432, 2432, 2436	1900	3000	6
1537WS: 1955 027 Four-Car Freight: 2065, 2046W, 3562 yellow, 3469, 6464-275, 6357	575	975	5
1538WS: 1955 027 Four-Car Passenger: 2065, 2046W, 2435, 2434, 2432, 2436	900	1500	6
1539W: 1955 027 Five-Car Freight: 2243 P/C A-B, 3620, 6446, 6561, 6560, 6419	900	1500	5
1541WS: 1955 027 Five-Car Freight: 2065, 2046W, 3482, 3461, 6415, 3494, 6427	600	1000	5
1542: 1956 027 Three-Car Freight: 520, 6014 red, 6012, 6017	200	375	4
1543: 1956 027 Three-Car Freight: 627, 6121, 6112, 6017	250	400	5
1545: 1956 027 Four-Car Freight: 628, 6424, 6014 red, 6257	300	500	6
1547S: 1956 027 Freight Hauler: 2018, 6026T, 6121, 6112, 6014 red, 6257	175	300	4
1549S: 1956 027 Three-Car Work Train: 1615, 1615T, 6262, 6560, 6119 orange	800	1350	5

1559W Five-Car Freight Set

1559W Five-Car Freight Set Boxed

#	Description	EX	LN	S
1551S: 1956 027 Four-Car Freight: 621, 6362, 6425, 6562, 6257		400	700	5
1552: 1956 027 Passenger: 629, 2434, 2432, 2436		1100	1900	7
1553W: 1956 027 Five-Car Freight: 2338, 6430, 6462 red, 6464-425, 6346, 6257		700	1100	5
1555WS: 027 Freight Hauler: 2018, 6026W, 3361, 6464-400, 6462 red, 6257		350	600	4
1557W: 1956 027 Five-Car Work Train: 621, 6436, 6511, 3620, 6560, 6119		500	950	5
1559W: 1956 027 Five-Car Freight: 2338, 6414, 3562 yellow, 6362, 3494-275, 6357		750	1200	5
1561WS: 1956 027 Five-Car Freight: 2065, 6026W, 6430, 3424, 6262, 6562, 6257		575	975	5
1562W: 1956 027 Four-Car Passenger: 2328, 2442, 2442, 2444, 2446		1800	3000	6
1563W: 1956 027 Five-Car Freight: 2240 P/C A-B, 6467, 3562 yellow, 3620, 6414, 6357		1700	2950	6
1565W: 1956 027 Five-Car Freight: 2065, 6026W, 3662, 3650, 6414, 6346, 6357		550	975	6

1957 Catalog

#	Description	EX	LN	S
1567W: 027 Five-Car Freight: 2243 P/C A-B, 3356,3424, 6672, 6430, 6357	975	1600	6
1569: 1957 027 Four-Car Freight: 202, 6014 white, 6111, 6112, 6017	300	500	4
1571: 1957 027 Five-Car Freight: 625, 6424, 6476, 6121, 6112, 6017	425	700	5
1573: 1957 027 Five-Car Freight: 250, 250T, 6025, 6112, 6464-425, 6476, 6017.	250	400	5
1575: 1957 027 Five-Car Freight: 205 P/T A-A, 6111, 6121, 6112, 6560, 6119.	350	600	5
1577S: 1957 027 Six-Car Freight: 2018, 1130T, 6121, 6464-475, 6111, 6014 red, 6112, 6017 . . .	250	400	5
1578S: 1957 027 Three-Car Passenger: 2018, 1130T, 2434, 2432, 2436	525	925	7
1579S: 1957 027 Seven-Car Freight: 2037, 1130T, 6111, 6025, 6476, 6468, 6112, 6121, 6017	300	500	5
1581: 1957 027 Seven-Car Freight: 611, 6476, 6024, 6424, 6464-650, 6025, 6560, 6119	550	975	5
1583WS: 1957 027 Six-Car Freight: 2037, 6026W, 6482, 6112, 6646, 6121, 6476 black, 6017	250	400	4

1587S Lady Lionel Pastel Train

1587S Lady Lionel boxes

# Description	EX	LN	S
1585W: 1957 027 Nine-Car Freight Train: 602, 6014 white, 6121, 6025, 6464-525, 6112, 6024, 6476 gray, 6111, 6017	425	700	5
1586: 1957 027 Three-Car Passenger: 204P/T A-A, 2432, 2432, 2436	700	1200	6
1587S: 1957-58 Lady Lionel Pastel Train Set: 2037-500, 1130T-500, 6462-500, 6464-515, 6436-500, 6464-510, 6427-500.	3000	5000	6
1589WS: 1957 027 Seven-Car Freight: 2037, 6026W, 6464-450, 6111, 6025 orange, 6024, 6424, 6112, 6017	500	750	5
1590: 1958 027 Four-Car Steam Freight: 249, 250T, 6014 red Bosco, 6151, 6112, 6017	300	500	4
1591: 1958 U.S. Marine Land & Sea Limited: 212, 6809, 6807, 6803, 6017-50.	1000	1700	6
1593: 1958 Five-Car UP Diesel Work Train: 613, 6476, 6818, 6660, 6112, 6119.	550	975	5
1595: 1958 027 Marine Battlefront Special: 1625, 1625T, 6804, 6808, 6806, 6017 gray.	1600	2700	7
1597S: 1958 027 Six-Car Coal King Smoking Freighter: 2018, 1130T, 6014 orange, 6818, 6476 red, 6025 black, 6112 blue, 6017	325	550	5

1600 Three-Car Burlington Passenger Set

# Description	EX	LN	S
1599: 1958 027 Six-Car Texas Special Freight: 210 A-A, 6801-50 w/yellow hull boat, 6112-1 black, 6014 orange Bosco or red Frisco, 6424-60, 6465-60 gray, 6017	400	775	4
1600: 1958 027 Three-Car Burlington Passenger: 216, 6572, 2432, 2436	950	1600	7
1601W: 1958 027 Five-Car Diesel Freight: 2337, 6800, 6464-425, 6801, 6810, 6017	900	1500	5
1603WS: 1958 027 Five-Car Whistling Mountain Climber Steam Freight: (2037, 6026W, 6424, 6014-60 white Bosco, 6818, 6112, 6017	375	700	5
1605W: 1958 027 Six-Car Santa Fe Diesel Freight: 208 AA, 6800, 6464-425, 6801, 6477, 6802, 6017.	900	1500	5
1607W: 1958 027 Six-Car Trouble Shooter Work Set: 2037, 6026W, 6465, 6818, 6464-425, 6112, 6660, 6119	475	800	5
1608W: 1958 027 Four-Car Merchants Limited Diesel Passenger: 209P/T A-A, 2434, 2432, 2432, 2436	1500	2500	7
1609: 1959-60 027 Three-Car Steam Freight: 246, 1130T, 6162-25 blue, 6476 red, 6057	125	200	2

1611 Four-car Alaskan Freight set

#	Description	EX	LN	S
1611: 1959 027 Four-Car Alaskan Freight: 614, 6825, 6162-50, 6465 black, 6027	575	950	4
1612: 1959-60 The General Old-Timer Outfit: 1862, 1862T, 1866, 1865	350	600	1
1613S: 1959 Four-Car B&O Steam Freight: 247, 247T, 6826, 6819, 6821, 6017	300	500	5
1615: 1959 Five-Car Boston & Maine Diesel Freight: 217P/C A-B, 6800, 6464-475, 6812, 6825, 6017-100	575	975	5
1617S: 1959 Five-Car Busy Beaver Steam Work Train: 2018, 1130T, 6816, 6536, 6812, 6670, 6119	825	1400	5
1619W: 1959 Five-Car Santa Fe Diesel Freight: 218P/T A-A, 6819, 6802, 6801, 6519, 6017-185 gray	425	800	4
1621WS: 1959 Five-Car Construction Special Steam Freight: 2037, 6026W, 6825, 6519, 6062, 6464-475, 6017	300	500	4
1623W: 1959 Five-Car NP Diesel Freight: 2349, 3512, 3435, 6424, 6062, 6017	1200	2000	7
1625WS: 1959 Five-Car Action King Steam Freight: 2037, 6026W, 6636, 3512, 6470, 6650, 6017 . . .	400	700	5

1639WS Six-Car Power House Special Steam Freight

1639WS Six-Car Power House Freight Set Boxed

#	Description	EX	LN	S
1626W: 1959 Four-Car Santa Fe Diesel Passenger: 208P/T A-A, 3428, 2412 blue stripe, 2412 blue stripe, 2416 blue stripe	750	1250	5
1627S: 1960 027 Three-Car Steam Freight: 244, 244T, 6062, 6825, 6017	90	150	1
1629: 1960 Four-Car C & O Diesel Freight: 225, 6650, 6470, 6819, 6219	300	500	1
1631WS: 1960 Four-Car Industrial Steam Freight: 243, 243W, 6519, 6812, 6465, 6017	300	500	2
1633: 1960 Land-Sea-Air Two-Unit Diesel Freight: 224P/C A-B, 6544, 6830, 6820, 6017-200	900	1500	4
1635WS: 1960 Five-Car Heavy-Duty Special Steam Freight: 2037, 243W, 6361, 6826, 6636, 6821, 6017...................................	450	850	5
1637W: 1960 Five-Car Twin Unit Diesel Freight: 218 P/T A-A, 6475, 6175, 6464-475, 6801, 6017-185	500	950	5
1639WS: 1960 Six-Car Power House Special Steam Freight: 2037, 243W, 6816, 6817, 6812, 6530, 6560, 6119	1750	2800	7

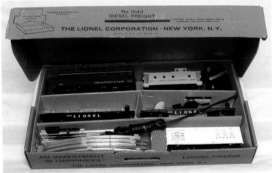

1643 Four-Car Sky-Scout Diesel Freight Set

#	Description	EX	LN	S
1640W: 1960 Five-Car Presidential Campaign Special: 218 P/T A-A, 3428, two 2412s blue stripe, 2416 blue stripe, 1640-100	650	1000	4
1641: 1961 Three-Car Headliner Steam Freight: 246, 244T, 3362, 6162, 6057	90	150	3
1642: 1961 Three-Car Circus Special Steam Freight: 244, 1130T, 3376, 6405, 6119	175	300	3
1643: 1961 Four-Car Sky-Scout Diesel Freight: 230, 3509, 6050, 6175, 6058	275	475	3
1644: 1961 Frontier Special General Passenger: 1862, 1862T, 3370, 1866, 1865	475	700	3
1645: 1961 027 Four-Car Diesel Freight: 229, 3410, 6465, 6825, 6059	240	400	4
1646: 1961 Four-Car Utility Steam Freight: 233, 233W, 6162, 6343, 6476 red, 6017.	350	600	2
1647: 1961 Freedom Fighter Missile Launcher Outfit: 45, 3665, 3519, 6830, 6448, 6814	900	1475	6
1648: 1961 Five-Car Supply Line Steam Freight: 2037, 233W, 6062, 6465, 6519, 6476 red, 6017 .	250	400	3

1810 Space Age Gift Pack

#	Description	EX	LN	S
1649: 1961 027 Five-Car Two-Unit Diesel Freight: 218P/C A-B, 6343, 6445, 6475, 6405, 6017 ...		525	900	6
1650: 1961 Five-Car Guardian Steam Freight: 2037, 233W, 6544, 6470, 3330, 3419, 6017		450	800	6
1651: 1961 Four-Car All Passenger Diesel: 218 P/T A-A, 2414 blue stripe, two 2412s blue stripe, 2416 blue stripe		750	1200	4
1800: 1959-60 The General Frontier Pack: 1862, 1862T, 1877, 1866, 1865, General Story Book .		400	675	3
1805: 1960 Land-Sea-And Air Gift Pack: 45, 3429, 3820, 6640, 6824		1750	3000	5
1809: 1961 The Western Gift Pack: 244, 1130T, 3370, 3376, 1877, 6017		300	500	3
1810: 1961 The Space Age Gift Pack: 231, 3665, 3519, 3820, 6017		550	975	3
2100: 1946 0 Gauge Three-Car Passenger: 224, 2466T, two brown 2442s, brown 2443		550	950	7
2100W: 1946 0 Gauge Three-Car Passenger: 224, 2466W, two brown 2442s, brown 2443		500	800	5

2105WS Three-Car Freight Outfit

# Description	EX	LN	S
2101: 1946 0 Gauge Three-Car Freight: 224, 2466T, 2555, 2452, 2457	400	675	6
2101W: 1946 0 Gauge Three-Car Freight: 224, 2466W, 2555, 2452, 2457	300	500	5
2103W: 1946 0 Gauge Four-Car Freight: 224, 2466W, 2458, 3559, 2555, 2457	425	1000	5
2105WS: 1946 Three-Car Freight Outfit: 671, 671W, 2555, 2454, 2457	400	1000	5
2110WS: 1946 Three-Car Passenger: 671, 671W, three 2625s.	1750	2975	7
2111WS: 1946 Four-Car Freight: 671, 671W, 3459, 2411, 2460, 2420	825	1400	7
2113WS: 1946 0 Gauge Three-Car Freight Outfit: 726, 2426W, 2855, 3854, 2457	2000	3200	7
2114WS: 1946 0 Gauge Three-Car Passenger Outfit: 726, 2426W, three 2625 "Irvington" Pullmans . .	2500	4000	6
2115WS: 1946 0 Gauge Four-Car Work Train with Smoke: 726, 2426W, 2458, 3451. 2460, 2420 . .	1350	2400	7
2120S: 1947 Three-Car De Luxe Passenger: 675, 2466T, two brown 2442s, brown 2443	500	875	6

2124W Three-Car Passenger Set

2124W Three-Car Passenger Set Boxed

#	Description	EX	LN	S
2120WS: 1947 Three-Car De Luxe Passenger: 675, 2466WX, two brown 2442s, brown 2443		525	900	4
2121S: 1947 Three-Car Freight: 675, 2466T, 2452, 2555, 2457		375	550	6
2121WS: 1947 Three-Car Freight: 675, 2466WX, 2452, 2555, 2457		400	575	5
2123WS: 1947 Four-Car Freight: 675, 2466WX, 2458, 3559, 2555, 2457		450	800	5
2124W: 1947 Three-Car Passenger: 2332, 2625 Irvington, 2625 Madison, 2625 Manhattan		3000	5000	5
2125WS: 1947 Four-Car Freight: 671, 671W, 2411, 2454, 2452, 2457		575	975	5
2126WS: 1947 Three-Car Passenger: 671, 671 W, 2625 Irvington, 2625 Madison, 2625 Manhattan.		1700	2900	5
2127WS: 1947 Lionel Work Train: 671, 671W, 3459, 2461, 2460, 2420		750	1250	5
2129WS: 1947 Four-Car Freight: 726, 2426W, 3854, 2411, 2855, 2457		2100	3500	6
2131WS: 1947 Four-Car De Luxe Work Train: 726, 2426W, 3462, 3451, 2460, 2420		1100	1900	5

2141WS Four car freight

#	Description	EX	LN	S
2133W: 1948 Twin Diesel O Gauge Freight: 2333 P/T A-A, 2458, 3459, 2555, 2357	1150	2000	5
2135WS: 1948 Three-Car Freight: 675, 2466WX, 2456, 2411, 2357	325	525	4
1949 Three-Car Freight: 675, 6466WX, 6456, 6411, 6457	300	500	4
2136WS: 1948 Three-Car Passenger: 675, 2466WX, two brown 2442s, brown 2443	550	900	5
1949 Three-Car Passenger: 675, 6466WX, two brown 6442s, brown 6443	500	850	4
2137WS: 1948 Four-Car De Luxe Freight: 675, 2466WX, 2458, 3459, 2456, 2357	400	700	4
2139W: 1948 Four-Car Freight: 2332, 3451, 2458, 2456, 2357	1500	2500	4
1948 0 Gauge Four-Car Freight Outfit: 2332, 6456, 3464, 3461, 6457	1400	2400	4
2140WS: 1948-49 Three-Car De Luxe Passenger: 671, 2671W, 2400, 2402, 2401	900	1500	5
2141WS: 1948 Four-Car Freight: 671, 2671W, 3451, 3462, 2456, 2357	500	775	4
1949 Four-Car Freight: 671, 2671W, 3461, 3472, 6456, 6457	500	775	4

2148WS Three-Car Deluxe Pullman Set

2148WS Three-Car Deluxe Pullman Set Boxed

#	Description	EX	LN	S
2143WS: 1948 Four-Car De Luxe Work Train: 671, 2671W, 3459, 2461, 2460, 2420		700	1200	5
2144W: 1948-49 Three-Car De Luxe Passenger Outfit: 2332, 2625, 2627, 2628		2400	4000	5
2145WS: 1948 Four-Car Freight: 726, 2426W, 3462, 2411, 2460, 2357		850	1400	5
2146WS: 1948-49 Three-Car Pullman: 726, 2426W, 2625, 2627, 2628		2400	4000	7
2147WS: 1949 Four-Car Freight Set: 675, 6466WX, 3472, 6465, 3469, 6457		350	600	3
2148WS: 1950 0 Gauge Three-Car Deluxe Pullman: 773, 2426W, 2625, 2627, 2628		4700	8500	6
2149B: 1949 0 Gauge Four-Car Diesel Work Train: 622, 6520, 3469, 2460, 6419		700	1100	5
2150WS: 1950 0 Gauge Deluxe Passenger: 681, 2671W, 2421, 2422, 2423		800	1300	5
2151W: 1949 0 Gauge Five-Car Diesel: 2333 P/T A-A, 3464, 6555, 3469, 6520, 6457		1100	1900	4
2153WS: 1949 Four-Car De Luxe Work Train: 671, 2671W, 3469, 6520, 2460, 6419		600	1000	4

2159W Five-Car Freight Set

2159W Five-Car Freight Set Boxed

# Description	EX	LN	S
2155WS: 1949 Four-Car Freight: 726, 2426W, 6411, 3656, 2460, 6457	800	1300	5
2159W: 1950 Five-Car Freight: 2330, 3464, 6462, 3461X, 6456, 6457	2000	3500	6
2161W: 1950 SF Twin Diesel Freight: 2343 A-A, 3469X, 3464, 3461X, 6520, 6457	1500	2500	4
2163WS: 1950 Four-Car Freight: 736, 2671WX, 6472, 6462, 6555, 6457	575	900	4
2163WS (Type II): 1951 Four-Car Freight: 736, 2671WX, 6472, 6462, 6465, 6457	550	875	4
2165WS: 1950 0 Gauge Four-Car Freight: 736, 2671WX, 3472, 6456, 3461X, 6457	600	1000	4
2167WS: 1950-51 Three-Car Freight: 681, 2671W, 6462, 3464, 6457	400	650	4
2169WS: 1950 Five-Car Freight w/smoke and whistle: 773, 2426W, 3656, 6456, 3469X, 6411, 6457	2700	4500	6
2171W: 1950 NYC Twin Diesel Freight: 2344 A-A, 3469X, 3464, 3461X, 6520, 6457	1200	2000	4

2179WS Three-Car Freight Set

# Description	EX	LN	S
2173WS: 1950 Four-Car Freight: 681, 2671W, 3472, 6555, 3469X, 6457	500	775	4
1951 Four-Car Freight: 681, 2671W, 3472, 6465, 3469X, 6457	500	775	4
2175W: 1950 Five-Car Santa Fe Twin Diesel Freight: 2343 A-A, 6456 black, 3464, 6555, 6462, 6457	1200	2000	3
1951 Five-Car Santa Fe Twin Diesel Freight: 2343 A-A, 6456 maroon, 3464, 6465, 6462, 6457	1200	2000	3
2177WS: 1952 Three-Car Freight: 675, 2046W, 6462, 6465, 6457	300	500	5
2179WS: 1952 Four-Car Freight: 671rr, 2046WX, 3464, 6465, 6462, 6457	400	700	4
2183WS: 1952 Four-Car Freight: 726rr, 2046W, 3464, 6462, 6465, 6457	550	900	4
2185W: 1950 Five-Car NYC Twin Diesel Freight: 2344 A-A, 6456 black, 3464, 6555, 6462, 6457	1200	2000	3
1951 Five-Car NYC Twin Diesel Freight: 2344 A-A, 6456 maroon, 3464, 6465, 6462, 6457	1200	2000	3
2187WS: 1952 Five-Car Freight: 671rr, 2046WX, 6462, 3472, 6456 maroon, 3469, 6457	500	850	5

2207W Triple-Diesel Freight Set

2207W Triple-Diesel Freight Set Boxed

#	Description	EX	LN	S
2189WS: 1952 Five-Car Transcontinental Fast Freight: 726rr, 2046W, 3520, 3656, 6462, 3461, 6457		600	1000	5
2190W: 1952 Four-Car Super Speedliner Passenger: 2343 A-A, 2533, 2532, 2534, 2531		1800	3000	3
1953 Four-Car Super Speedliner Passenger: 2353 A-A, 2533, 2532, 2534, 2531		1800	3000	3
2191W: 1952 Four-Car Diesel Freight: 2343 A-A, 2343C B Unit, 6462, 6656, 6456, 6457		1500	2500	4
2193W: 1952 Four-Car Diesel Freight: 2344 A-A, 2344C B-Unit, 6462, 6656, 6456, 6457		1600	2650	4
2201WS (Type I): 1953 Four-Car Freight: 685. 6026W, 6462, 6464-50, 6465, 6357		750	1200	5
2201WS (Type II): 1954 Four-Car Freight: 665, 6026W, 6462, 6464-50, 6465, 6357		650	1100	4
2203WS: 1953 Four-Car Freight: 681, 2046WX, 3520, 6415, 6464-25, 6417		725	1200	4
2205WS: 1953 Five-Car Freight: 736, 2046W, 3484, 6415, 6468 blue, 6456, 6417		700	1150	4
2207W: 1953 Triple Diesel Freight: 2353 A-A, 2343C B Unit, 3484, 6415, 6462, 6417		1500	2500	4

2209W Triple-Diesel Freight Set

2209W Triple-Diesel Freight Set Boxed

# Description	EX	LN	S
2209W: 1953 Triple Diesel Freight: 2354 AA, 2344C B Unit, 3484, 6415, 6462, 6417	1550	2600	4
2211WS: 1953 Four-Car Freight: 681, 2046WX, 3656, 3461, 6464-75, 6417.	700	1200	5
2213WS: 1953 Five-Car Freight: 736, 2046W, 3461, 3520, 3469, 6460, 6419	575	975	4
2217WS: 1954 0 Gauge Four-Car Freight: 682, 2046WX, 3562 gray, 6464-175, 6356, 6417. . . .	1000	1600	5
2219W: 1954 Five-Car Fairbanks-Morse Power Giant Freight: 2321, 6415, 6462 green, 6464-50, 6456 gray, 6417	1200	2000	5
2221WS: 1954 0 Gauge Five-Car Freight: 646, 2046W, 3620, 3469. 6468 blue, 6456 gray, 6417.	600	1000	4
2222WS: 1954 0 Gauge Three-Car Pullman: 646, 2046W, 2530, 2532, 2531	1600	2700	5
2223W: 1954 0 Gauge Five-Car Freight: 2321, 3482, 3461, 6464-100, 6462 red, 6417.	2400	4000	6
2225WS: 1954 Five-Car Work Freight: 736, 2046W, 3461, 3620, 3562 gray, 6460 black cab, 6419 . . .	750	1200	5

2243W O-Gauge Five-Car Freight Set

2243W O-Gauge Five-Car Freight Set Boxed

#	Description	EX	LN	S
2227W: 1954 0 Gauge Five-Car Freight: 2353 A-A, 3562 gray, 6356, 6456 red, 6468 blue, 6417	1500	2500	4
2229W: 1954 0 Gauge Five-Car Freight: 2354 A-A, 3562 gray, 6356, 6456 red, 6468 blue, 6417	1500	2500	5
2231W: 1954 0 Gauge Five-Car Freight: 2356 A-A, 2356C B Unit, 6561, 6511, 3482, 6415, 6417 . .	2400	4000	5
2234W: 1954 Four-Car Super-Streamliner: 2353 A-A, 2530, 2532, 2533, 2531.	2200.	3800	4
2235W: 1955 0 Gauge Four-Car Freight: 2338, 6436, 6362, 6560 red, 6419	550	900	3
2237WS: 1955 0 Gauge Three-Car Freight: 665, 6026W, 3562 yellow, 6415, 6417	400	750	3
2239W: 1955 0 Gauge Streak-Liner: 2363 P/C A-B, 6672, 6464-125, 6414, 6517.	1800	3000	5
2241WS: 1955 0 Gauge Freight Snorter: 646, 2046W, 3359, 6446, 3620, 6417.	600	1000	5
2243W: 1955 0 Gauge Five-Car Freight: 2321, 3662, 6511, 6462 red, 6464-300, 6417.	1500	2500	5
2244W: 1955 Three-Car Passenger: 2367 P/C A-B, 2530, 2533, 2531	4000	6500	6

2257WS O-Gauge Five-Car Freight Set

#	Description	EX	LN	S
2245WS: 1955 0 Gauge Five-Car Freight: 682, 2046W, 3562, 6436, 6561, 6560, 6419		800	1250	5
2247W: 1955 0 Gauge Five-Car Freight: 2367 P/C A-B, 6462 red, 3662, 6464-150, 3361, 6517 . . .		2500	4000	5
2249WS: 1955 0 Gauge Five-Car Freight: 736, 2046W, 3359, 3562 yellow, 6414, 6464-275, 6517		900	1500	5
2251W: 1955 0 Gauge Five-Car Freight: 2331, 3359, 3562 yellow, 6414, 6464-275, 6517		2500	4000	5
2253W: 1955 0 Gauge Five-Car Freight: 2340-25 green, 3620, 6414, 3361, 6464-300, 6417.		2700	4500	5
2254W: 1955 The Congressional: 2340-1 Tuscan, 2544, 2543, 2542, 2541		5500	9500	5
2255W: 1956 0 Gauge Four-Car Work Train: 601, 3424, 6362, 6560, 6119 orange.		600	1000	4
2257WS: 1956 0 Gauge Five-Car Freight: 665, 2046W, 3361, 6346, 6467, 6462 red, 6427		500	750	3
2259W: 1956 0 Gauge Five-Car Freight: 2350, 6464-425, 6430, 3650, 6511, 6427		850	1400	3

2263W O-Gauge Five-Car Freight Set

#	Description	EX	LN	S
2261WS: 1956 0 Gauge Freight Hauler: 646, 2046W, 3562 yellow, 6414, 6436, 6376, 6417...		575	950	5
2263W: 1956 0 Gauge Five-Car Freight: 2350, 3359, 6468, 6414, 3662, 6517		900	1500	5
2265WS: 1956 0 Gauge Five-Car Freight: 736, 2046W, 3620, 6430, 3424, 6467, 6517		750	1200	5
2267W: 1956 Five-Car Freight: 2331, 3562 yellow, 3359, 3361, 6560, 6419		1600	2650	5
2269W: 1956 0 Gauge Five-Car Freight: 2368 P/C A-B, 3356, 6518, 6315, 3361, 6517		4000	6750	7
2270W: 1956 Three-Car Jersey Central Passenger: 2341, 2533, 2532, 2531		5600	9000	7
2271W: 1956 0 Gauge Five-Car Freight: 2360-25 green, 3424, 3662, 6414, 6418, 6417		3000	5000	5
2273W: 1956 Six-Car Milwaukee Road Diesel Freight: 2378P/C A-B, 342, 6342, 3562 yellow, 3662, 3359, 6517		4000	6500	6
2274W: 1956 The Great Congressional: 2360-1 Tuscan, 2544, 2543, 2542, 2541		5000	8500	7

2291W Super O-Gauge Five-Car Freight Set

2291W Super O-Gauge Five-Car Freight Set Boxed

#	Description	EX	LN	S
2275W: 1957 0 Gauge Four-Car Freight: 2339, 3444, 6464-475, 6425, 6427.		750	1200	3
2276W: 1957 Budd RDC Commuter Set: 404, 2559, 2559.		3000	5000	5
2277WS: 1957 0 Gauge Four-Car Work Train: 665, 2046W, 3650, 6446, 6560, 6119.		550	900	5
2279W: 1957 0 Gauge Five-Car Freight: 2350, 6464-425, 6424, 3424, 6477, 6427.		825	1300	4
2281W: 1957 0 Gauge Five-Car Freight: 2243 A-B, 3562 orange, 6464-150, 3361, 6560, 6119		1200	2000	3
2283WS: 1957 0 Gauge Five-Car Freight: 646, 2046W, 3424, 3361, 6464-525, 6562 black, 6357.		600	1000	5
2285W: 1957 0 Gauge Five-Car Freight: 2331, 6418, 6414, 3662, 6425, 6517		1800	3000	6
2287W: 1957 0 Gauge Five-Car Freight: 2351, 342, 6342, 6464-500, 3650, 6315, 6427.		1800	3000	6
2289WS: 1957 Super 0 Five-Car Freight: 736, 2046W, 3359, 3494-275, 3361, 6430, 6427		750	1250	5
2291W: 1957 Super 0 Five-Car Freight: 2379 P/C A-B, 3562 orange, 3530, 3444, 6464-525, 6657.		3000	5000	6

2297WS 16 Wheeler Class J Set

2297WS 16 Wheeler Class J Set

#	Description	EX	LN	S
2292WS: 1957 Super O Steam Luxury Liner: 646, 2046W, 2530, 2533, 2532, 2531		1500	2500	4
2293W: 1957 Five-Car Freight: 2360 Tuscan, 3662, 3650, 6414, 6518, 6417		2900	4900	6
2295WS: 1957 Six-Car Steam Freight: 746, 746W, 342, 6342, 3530, 3361, 6560, 6419-100		3000	5000	7
2296W: 1957 Super 0 Diesel Luxury Liner: 2373 P/T A-A, 2552, 2552, 2552, 2551		6000	10000	6
2297WS: 1957 The 16 Wheeler Class J: 746, 746W, 264, 6264, 3356, 345, 6342, 3662, 6517		3300	5500	7
2501W: 1958 Super O Work Train: 2348, 6464-525, 6802, 6560, 6119		800	1200	5
2502W: 1958 Super O Rail-Diesel Commuter: 400, 2559, 2550		1800	3000	7
2503WS: 1958 Timberland Special Freight: 665, 2046W, 3361, 6434, 6801, 6536, 6357		550	950	5
2505W: 1958 Super 0 Five-Car Freight: 2329, 6805, 6519, 6800, 6464-500, 6357.		1500	2500	5

2507W Super O Five-Car Diesel Freight Set

#	Description	EX	LN	S
2507W: 1958 Super 0 Five-Car Diesel Freight: 2242P/C A-B, 3444, 6464-425, 6424. 6468-25, 6357	2000	3000	6
2509WS: 1958 The Owl Five-Car Freight: 665, 2046W, 6414, 3650, 6464-475, 6805, 6357	800	1200	5
2511W: 1958 Super 0 Five-Car Electric Work Train: 2352, 3562 orange, 3424, 3361, 6560, 6119	1200	2000	6
2513W: 1958 Super 0 Six-Car Freight Train: 2329, 6556, 6425, 6414, 6434, 3359, 6427-60	2000	3500	7
2515WS: 1958 Five-Car Mainliner Steam Freight: 646, 2046W, 3662, 6424, 3444, 6800, 6427	825	1350	5
2517W: 1958 Super 0 Five-Car Diesel Freight: 2379 A-B, 6519, 6805, 6434, 6800, 6657	2400	4000	7
2518W: 1958 Super 0 Three-Car Passenger: 2352, 2533, 2534, 2531	1500	2500	6
2519W: 1958 Super 0 Six-Car Diesel Freight: 2331, 6434, 3530, 6801, 6414, 6464-275, 6557	1900	3000	5
2521WS: 1958 Super 0 Six-Car Freight: 746, 746W, 6805, 3361, 6430, 3356, 6557	2400	4000	6

2531WS Super O Five Car Steam Freight

2531WS Super O Five Car Steam Freight boxes

#	Description	EX	LN	S
2523W: 1958 Super O Super Chief Freight: 2383 A-A, 264, 6264, 6434, 6800, 3662, 6517		1800	3000	6
2525WS: 1958 Super 0 Six-Car Work Train: 746, 746W, 345, 342, 6519, 6518, 6560, 6419-100 . .		3000	5000	7
2526W: 1958 Super Chief Passenger: 2383 P/T A-A, 2530, 2532, 2532, 2531		1800	3000	4
2527: 1959-60 Super O Missile Launcher Outfit: 44, 3419, 6844, 6823, 6814, 943.		700	1200	4
2528WS: 1959-61 Five-Star Frontier Special Outfit: 1872, 1872T, 1877, 1876, 1875W		750	1250	3
2529W: 1959 Five-Car Virginian Rectifier Work Train: 2329, 3512, 6819, 6812, 6560, 6119. . . . :		1200	2000	5
2531WS: 1959 Super O Five-Car Steam Freight: 637, 2046W, 3435, 6817, 6636, 6825, 6119		1200	2000	6
2533W: 1959 Five-Car Great Northern Electric Freight: 2358, 6650, 6414, 3444, 6470, 6357 . . .		1800	3000	7
2535WS: 1959 Super 0 Five-Car Hudson Steam Freight: 665, 2046W, 3434, 6823, 3672, 6812, 6357		1000	1600	5

2545W Six-Car N&W Space-Freight Set

2545W Six-Car N&W Space-Freight Set Boxed

# Description	EX	LN	S
2537W: 1959 Five-Car New Haven Diesel Freight: 2242 P/C A-B, 3435, 3650, 6464-275, 6819, 6427	2400	4000	7
2539WS: 1959 Five-Car Hudson Steam Freight: 665, 2046W, 3361, 464, 6464-825, 3512, 6812, 6357	1500	2500	6
2541W: 1959 Five-Car Super Chief Freight: 2383 P/T A-A, 3356, 3512, 6519, 6816, 6427	2300	3900	6
2543WS: 1959 Six-Car Berkshire Steam Freight: 736, 2046W, 264, 6264, 3435, 6823, 6434, 6812, 6557	2000	3500	7
2544W: 1959-60 Four-Car Super Chief Streamliner: 2383 P/T A-A, 2530, 2563, 2562, 2561	4000	6500	6
2545WS: 1959 Six-Car N&W Space-Freight: 746, 746W, 175, 6175, 6470, 3419, 6650, 3540, 6517.	3000	5000	6
2547WS: 1960 Four-Car Variety Special Steam Freight: 637, 2046W, 3330, 6475, 6361, 6357	600	1000	5
2549W: 1960 A Mighty Military Diesel Outfit: 2349, 3540, 6470, 6819, 6650, 3535	1200	2000	3
2551W: 1960 Six-Car Great Northern Diesel Freight: 2358, 6828, 3512, 6827, 6736, 6812, 6427	2100	3000	6

2574 Five-Car Defender Diesel Freight

2574 Five-Car Defender Diesel Freight boxes

# Description	EX	LN	S
2553WS: 1960 The Majestic Berkshire Five-Car Freight: 736, 2046W, 3830, 3435, 3419, 3672, 6357	1500	2500	5
2555W: 1960 Over & Under Twin Railroad Empire: 2383 P/T A-A, 3434, 3366, 6414, 6464-900, 6357-50, 110-85 as well as corresponding units in HO. Popularly known as the "father and son set."	8000	12000	8
2570: 1961 Five-Car Husky Diesel Freight: 616, 6822, 6828, 6812, 6736, 6130	550	900	4
2571: 1961 Fort Knox Special Steam Freight: 637, 736W, 3419, 6445, 6361, 6119	600	1000	5
2572: 1961 Five-Car Space Age Diesel Freighter: 2359, 6544, 3830, 6448, 3519, 3535	800	1350	4
2573: 1961 Five-Car TV Special Steam Freight: 736, 736W, 3545, 6416, 6475, 6440, 6357	1200	2000	5
2574: 1961 Five-Car Defender Diesel Freight: 2383 P/T A-A, 3665, 3419, 448, 6448, 3830, 6437	1800	3000	5
2575: 1961 Seven-Car Dynamo Electric Freight: 2360 single stripe, 6530, 6828, 6464-900, 6827, 6560, 6437	3000	5000	7

4110WS Lionel Electric Railroad Set

4110WS Lionel Electric Railroad Set

#	Description	EX	LN	S
2576: 1961 Four-Car Super Chief Streamline: 2383 P/T A-A, 2563, 2562, 2562, 2561	4000	6500	6
4109WS: 1946-47 Electronic Control Set: 671R, 4671W, 4452, 4454, 5459, 4457.	900	1500	5
4110WS: 1948-49 Lionel Electronic Railroad: 671R, 4671W, 4452, 4454, 5459, 4357, 97, 151	2000	3700	7
11201: 1962 Fast Starter Steam Freight: 242, 1060T, 6042-75, 6502, 6047	90	150	1
11212: 1962 Four-Unit Cyclone Diesel Freight: 633, 3349, 6825, 6057	225.	350	2
11222: 1962 Five-Unit VagA-Bond Steam Freight: 236, 1050T, 3357, 6343, 6119	125	200	3
11232: 1962 027 Five-Unit Diesel Freight: 232, 3410, 6062, 6413, 6057-50 orange	425	700	6
11242: 1962 Trail Blazer Steam Freight: 233, 233W, 6465, 6476 red, 6162, 6017	80	125	2
11252: 1962 027 Seven-Unit Diesel Freight: 211 A-A, 3509, 6448, 3349, 6463,			
11268: 1962 027 Six-Unit Diesel Freight: 2365, 3619, 3470, 3349, 6501, 6017.	900	1500	4

11288 Seven-Unit Orbiter Diesel Freight Set

#	Description	EX	LN	S
11278: 1962 Seven-Unit Plainsman Steam Freight: 2037, 233W, 6473, 6162, 6050-110, 6825, 6017		250	400	4
11288: 1962 Seven-Unit Orbiter Diesel Freight: 229 P/C A-B, 3413, 6512, 6413, 6463, 6059		750	1200	5
11298: 1962 Seven-Unit Vigilant Steam Freight: 2037, 233W, 3419, 6544, 6448, 3330, 6017		400	650	5
11308: 1962 027 Six-Unit Diesel Passenger: 218 P/T A-A, 2414, two 2412s, 2416		600	1000	4
11311: 1963 Value Packed Steam Freight: 1062, 1061T, 6409-25, 6076-100, 6167		90	150	2
11321: 1963 027 Five-Unit Diesel Freighter: 221, 3309, 6076-75, 6042-75, 6167-50 yellow		250	400	3
11331: 1963 Outdoorsman Steam Freight: 242, 1060T, 6473, 6476-25, 6142, 6059-50		125	200	2
11341: 1963 Space-Prober Diesel Freight: 634, 3410, 6407, 6014-335 white, 6463, 6059-50		950	1600	6
11351: 1963 Land Rover Steam Freight: 237, 1060T, 6050-100, 6465-100, 6408, 6162, 6119-100		200	350	3

11430 Five-Unit Steam Freight Set

# Description	EX	LN	S
11361: 1963 Shooting Star Diesel Freight: 211 P/T A-A, 3665-100, 3413-150, 6470, 6413, 6257-100	750	1250	6
11375: 1963 Cargomaster Steam Freight: 238, 234W, 6822-50, 6414-150, 6465-150, 6476-75, 6162, 6257-100	650.	1100	5
11385: 1963 Space Conqueror Diesel Freight: 223P/218C A-B, 3619-100, 3470-100, 3349-100, 6407, 6257-100	1800	3000	6
11395: 1963 Muscleman Steam Freight: 2037, 234W, 6464-725, 6469-50, 6536, 6440-50, 6560-50, 6119-100	600	1000	5
11405: 1963 027 Six-Unit Diesel Passenger: 218 A-A, 2414, two 2412s, 2416	700	1125	4
11420: 1964 Four-Unit Steam Freight: 1061, 1061T, 6042-250, 6167-25	75	125	2
11430: 1964 Five-Unit Steam Freight: 1062,1061T, 6176, 6142, 6167-125	90	150	2
11440: 1964 Five-Unit Diesel Freight: 221, 3309, 6176-50 black, 6142-125 blue, 6167-100 red	200	350	2
11450: 1964 Six-Unit Steam Freight: 242, 1060T, 6473, 6142-75 green, 6176-50 black, 6059-50.	150	250	2

11480 Seven Diesel Freight

11490 Five-Unit Diesel Passenger

#	Description	EX	LN	S
11460: 1964 Seven-Unit Steam Freight: 238, 234W, 6014-335 white, 6465-150 orange, 6142-100 blue, 6176-75 yellow, 6119-100	125	200	3
11470: 1964 Seven-Unit Steam Freight: 237, 1060T, 6014-335 white, 6465-150 orange, 6142-100 blue, 6176-50 yellow, 6119-100	180	300	5
11480: 1964 Seven-Unit Diesel Freight: 213 P/T A-A, 6473, 6176-50 black, 6142-150, 6014-335 white, 6257-100	600	1000	5
11490: 1964-65 Five-Unit Diesel Passenger: 212 P/T A-A, 2404, 2405, 2406	600	1000	4
11500: 1964 Seven-Unit Steam Freight: 2029, 234W, 6465-150 orange, 6402-50, 6176-75 yellow, 6014-335 white, 6257-100	250	400	4
1965 Seven-Unit Steam Freight: 2029, 234W, 6465-150 orange, 6402-50, 6176 black, 6014-335 white, 6059	250	400	4
1966 Seven-Unit Steam Freight: 2029, 234W, 6465-150 orange, 6402-50, 6176-75 yellow, 6014-335 white, 6059	250	400	4
11510: 1964 Seven-Unit Steam Freight: 2029, 1060T, 6465-150 orange, 6402-50, 6176-75 yellow, 6014-335 white, 6257-100	275	450	4
11520: 1965-66 Six-Unit Steam Freight: 242,1062T, 6176, 3364, 6142, 6059	100	175	2

11590 Five-Unit Illuminated Passenger

#	Description	EX	LN	S
11530: 1965-66 Five-Unit Diesel Freight: 634, 6014-335 white, 6142, 6402, 6130		175	300	2
11540: 1965-66 Six-Unit Steam Freight: 239, 242T, 6473, 6465, 6176, 6119		175	300	5
11550: 1965-66 Six-Unit Steam Freight: 239, 234W, 6473, 6465, 6176, 6119		225	375	4
11560: 1965-66 Seven-Unit Diesel Freight: 211 P/T A-A, 6473, 6176, 6142, 6465, 6059		250	400	2
11590: 1966 Five-Unit Illuminated Passenger: 212 P/T A-A, 2408, 2409, 2410		700	1100	4
11600: 1968 Seven-Unit Steam Freight: 2029, 234W, 6014-335 white, 6476 yellow, 6315, 6560, 6130		750	1250	5
11710: 1969 Five-Unit Steam Freight: 1061, 1062T, 6402, 6142, 6059		125	200	3
11720: 1969 Five-Unit Diesel Freight: 2024, 6142, 6402, 6176 yellow, 6057 brown		200	325	5
11730: 1969 Six-Unit Diesel Freight: 645, 6402, 6014-85 orange, 6142, 6176 black, 6167		300	500	4

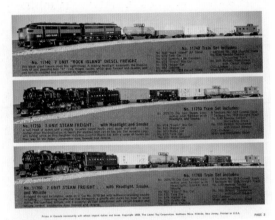

1969 Catalog

#	Description	EX	LN	S
11740: 1969 Seven-Unit Diesel Freight: 2041 A-A, 6315, 6142, 6014-410 white, 6476 yellow, 6057 brown.................................		325	550	5
11750: 1969 Seven-Unit Steam Freight: 2029, 234T, 6014-85 orange, 6476 black, 6473, 6315, 6130.		500	750	6
11760: 1969 Seven-Unit Steam Freight: 2029, 234W, 6014-410 white, 6315, 6476 black, 3376, 6119.................................		300	500	4
12502: 1962 Prairie-Rider Gift Pack: 1862, 1862T, 3376, 1877, 1866, 1865		600	1000	5
12512: 1962 Enforcer Gift Pack: 45, 3413, 3619, 3470, 3349, 6017		900	1500	5
12700: 1964 Seven-Unit Steam Freight: This set was identical to the 1964 12710 listed below, but did not include a transformer..................		900	1500	5
12710: 1964 Seven-Unit Steam Freight: 736, 736W, 6464-725, 6162-100 blue, 6414-75, 6476-135 yellow, 6437		925	1550	5
12710: 1965-66 Seven-Unit Steam Freight: 736, 736W, 6464-725, 6162-100 blue, 6414, 6476-135 yellow, 6437.........................		925	1550	5

12780 Six-Unit Diesel Passenger Set

12780 Six-Unit Diesel Passenger Set Boxed

# Description	EX	LN	S
12720: 1964 Seven-Unit Diesel Freight: This set was identical to the 1964 12730 listed below, but did not include a transformer.	1500	2500	5
12730: 1964 Seven-Unit Diesel Freight: 2383 P/T A-A, 6464-725, 6162-100 blue, 6414-75, 6476-135 yellow, 6437.	1500	2500	5
12730: 1965-66 Seven-Unit Diesel Freight: 2383 P/T A-A, 6464-725, 6162-100 blue, 6414, 6476-135 yellow, 6437.	1500	2500	5
12740: 1964 Nine-Unit Diesel Freight: This set was identical to the 1964 12750 listed below, but did not include a transformer.	1500	2500	6
12750: 1964 Nine-Unit Diesel Freight: 2383 P/T A-A, 3662, 6822, 6361, 6464-525, 6436-110, 6315-60, 6437	1500	2500	6
12760: 1964 Nine-Unit Steam Freight: This set was identical to the 1964 12770 listed below, but did not include a transformer.	1500	2500	6
12770: 1964 Nine-Unit Steam Freight: 736, 736W, 3662, 6822, 6361, 6464-525, 6436-110, 6315-60, 6437.	1500	2500	6
12780: 1964-66 Six-Unit Diesel Passenger: 2383 P/T A-A, 2523, 2522, 2523, 2521	3300	5500	5

13008 Six-Unit Champion Steam Freight Set

# Description	EX	LN	S
12800: 1965-66 Six-Unit Diesel Freight: 2346, 6428, 6436-110, 6464-475, 6415, 6017	600	1000	3
12820: 1965 Eight-Unit Diesel Freight: 2322, 3662, 6822, 6361, 6464-725, 6436-110, 6315, 6437 . .	1500	2500	5
12840: 1966 Seven-Unit Steam Freight: 665, 736W, 6464-375, 6464-450, 6431, 6415, 6437	900	1600	5
12850: 1966 Eight-Unit Diesel Freight: 2322, 3662, 6822, 6361, 6464-725, 6436-110, 6315, 6437 . .	1500	2500	5
13008: 1962 Six-Unit Champion Steam Freight: 637, 736W, 3349, 6448, 6501, 6119	400	650	5
13018: 1962 Six-Unit Starfire Diesel Freight: 616, 6500, 6650, 3519, 6448, 6017-235	1200	2000	6
13028: 1962 Six-Unit Defender Diesel Freight: 2359, 3665, 3349, 3820, 3470, 6017-100	900	1500	3
13036: 1962 Six-Unit Plainsman Steam Outfit: 1872, 1872T, 6445, 3370, 1876, 1875W	900	1500	4
13048: 1962 Seven-Unit Steam Freight: 736, 736W, 6822, 6414, 3362, 6440, 6437	800	1400	3

13078 Five-Unit Presidential Passenger Set

13078 Five-Unit Presidential Passenger Set Boxed

#	Description	EX	LN	S
13058: 1962 Seven-Unit Vanguard Diesel Freight: 2383 P/T A-A, 3619, 3413, 6512, 470, 6470, 6437		1600	2700	4
13068: 1962 Eight-Unit Goliath Electric Freight: 2360 single stripe, 6464-725, 6828, 6416, 6827, 6530, 6475, 6437		3000	5000	7
13078: 1962 Five-Unit Presidential Passenger: 2360 single stripe, 2523, 2522, 2522, 2521		3600	6000	6
13088: 1962 Six-Unit Presidential Passenger: 2383 P/T A-A, 2523, 2522, 2522, 2521		2500	4200	5
13098: 1963 Goliath Steam Freight: 637, 736W, 6469, 6464-900, 6414, 6446, 6447		2000	3600	6
13108: 1963 Super 0 Seven-Unit Diesel Freight: 617, 3665, 3419, 6448, 3830, 3470, 6119-100		900	1500	5
13118: 1963 Super 0 Eight-Unit Steam Freight: 736, 736W, 6446-60, 6827, 3362, 6315-60, 6560, 6429		1500	2500	5
13128: 1963 Super 0 Seven-Unit Diesel Freight: 2383 P/T A-A, 3619, 3413, 6512, 448, 6448, 6437		1800	3000	6

13150 Nine-Unit Freight

#	Description	EX	LN	S
13138: 1963 Majestic Electric Freight: 2360 single stripe, 6464-725, 6828, 6416, 6827, 6315-60, 6436-110, 6437		3000	5000	6
13148: 1963 Super Chief Passenger: 2383 P/T A-A, 2523, 2523, 2522, 2521		2400	4000	5
13150: 1964 Super 0 Nine-Unit Steam Freight: 773, 736W, 3434, 6361, 3662, 6415, 3356, 6436-110, 6437...................................		3000	5000	7
1965-66 Super 0 Nine-Unit Steam Freight: 773, 773W, 3434, 6361, 3662, 6415, 3356, 6436-110, 6437...................................		3000	5000	7

Lionel Catalogs and Paper Products

For many, the collecting of Lionel paper goods is a hobby unto itself. Indeed, so vast was Lionel's production of trains, it is difficult to comprehend that in fact there were more different paper products produced than trains themselves. A large display area indeed is required to display a "complete"—whatever that means—collection of both.

Beyond the celebrated color consumer catalog, during the later portion of the prewar era Lionel published a dealer advance catalog. Though often similar to the consumer catalog, dealer catalogs also illustrated store displays and promotional items that were not shown in the regular catalog. Also, these dealer catalogs often give us insight into how pieces evolved, for the illustrations in the dealer publication were often based on pre-production samples. Some items are shown that were never produced.

Far from the full-color 1942 catalog full of trains that closed the prewar era, the 1900 Lionel catalog was black and white, and illustrated no trains at all.

Virtually every operating piece Lionel produced had its own instructional document, often several editions as production continued on good selling items.

Booklets were printed for department store and hobby shop salespeople, teaching the "right" way to extol the virtues of Lionel's products.

Rather than trying to list and illustrate each paper product issued, which would require a massive volume, these listings will be confined to catalogs: consumer, dealer and accessory. A few other items of special interest are listed as well.

Unlike the trains, only two values are listed for paper products, New and Excellent. Paper in less than excellent condition is not generally considered collectible. Beware, however, that like the trains, rare and valuable catalogs have been reproduced, and those that are not marked as such are sometimes hard to distinguish.

1945 Consumer catalog: Lionel rushed an outfit on the market to meet the pent-up demand for trains caused by the war years. Only one type of outfit was available in 1945, and Lionel knew it could not meet the demand. Nevertheless, a four-page 8 1/2 x 11- brochure was produced extolling the return of Lionel Trains, with new features, too. The company hoped to continue fanning the flames of desire among consumers until production could meet demand. The strategy worked.

Ex	N	Rarity
150	225	8

1946 Advance catalog: 24-page 10 1/2 x 8 5/16 horizontal format catalog with cover reading "World's Finest Lionel Trains for 1946."

Ex	N	Rarity
200	325	8

1946 Consumer Catalog: 16-page 8 3/8 x 11 1/4 horizontal format catalog.

Ex	N	Rarity
40	65	6

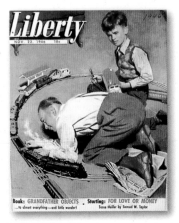

1946 Liberty Magazine: Lionel, concerned about distribution problems for its catalog, took out one of the most expensive advertisements of anyone up to that time. A 16-page insert, duplicating the consumer catalog, was put in the November 23, 1946, edition of *Liberty* magazine.

Ex	N	Rarity
100	175	7

1946 Scenic Effects for Model Railroads: 24-page, 6 x 9 booklet promoting Lionel products and describing how to build a layout.

Ex	N	Rarity
20	30	5

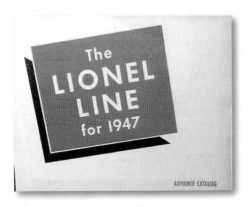

1947 Advance Catalog: 14 x 11, 22-page vertical format catalog. The cover reads "The Lionel Line for 1947."

Ex	N	Rarity
185	275	7

1947 Consumer Catalog: Various versions of this 32-page color horizontal format catalog were printed. All were trying to get the price and description of the new GG1 locomotive correct, and today all are equally valued.

Ex	N	Rarity
45	80	5

1947 Fun With Model Railroading: 32-page booklet with red cover. This details various scenic techniques and operating ideas for a Lionel layout.

Ex	N	Rarity
20	30	4

1948 Advance Catalog: 14 x 11 20-page horizontal format catalog. Interestingly, the 1948 F3 diesels were not shown in the advance catalog.

Ex	N	Rarity
175	250	7

1948 Consumer Catalog: 11 1/8 x 8 36-page horizontal format catalog with a Pennsylvania S2 turbine on the cover.

Ex	N	Rarity
50	75	5

1948 3-D Poster: 18 x 19 red and blue-printed poster of Lionel Trains. Came with celluloid 3-D glasses as an insert in some of the 1948 consumer catalogs.

Ex	N	Rarity
20	40	6

1948 Make These Realistic Models For Your Lionel Railroad: 23 1/4 x 25 printed sheet of cut-out structures printed in red, green, and blue ink.

Ex	N	Rarity
45	65	6

1948 For the Man Who Sells Lionel Trains: This was a training booklet for Lionel retailers.

Ex	N	Rarity
75	150	8

1949 Consumer Catalog: 11 1/4 x 8, 38-page horizontal format catalog. The cover illustration is of a family admiring a fantastic Lionel display. There are several minor variations of this catalog, most having to do with the 6220 locomotive on page 11, but these variations don't affect values.

Ex	N	Rarity
150	225	7

1949 Track Layout Planning Book for Pop: A 16-page, 5 1/8 x 7 1/16-inch booklet of various track configurations. A pipe-smoking father figure is on the front cover.

Ex	N	Rarity
20	35	5

1950 Consumer Catalog: 11 1/4 x 8, 44-page horizontal format full-color catalog.

Ex	N	Rarity
60	100	5

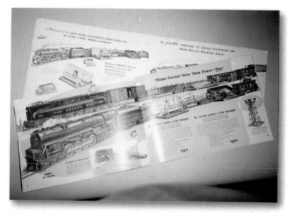

1950 Replacement Catalog: This 40-page 11 x 8 horizontal format catalog was issued when the supply of four-color catalogs was exhausted. It was printed in red and black ink.

Ex	N	Rarity
100	150	7

1950 Lionel Railroading is Fun: 17 1/4 x 23 poster printed in green and black ink with layout ideas.

Ex	N	Rarity
10	20	4

1951 Advance Catalog: 11 x 8, 24-page advance catalog with red and black cover.

Ex	N	Rarity
40	75	6

1951 Consumer Catalog: 11 1/8 x 7 3/4, 36-page horizontal format full-color catalog.

Ex	N	Rarity
30	60	4

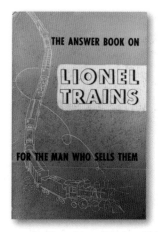

1951 The Answer Book on Lionel Trains: This was a 5 1/2 x 8 1/2, 34-page training booklet for Lionel retailers.

Ex	N	Rarity
60	80	7

1951 Romance of Model Railroading: 9 x 6, 32-page orange-covered booklet lavishly illustrated with photos of the Lionel showroom layout.

Ex	N	Rarity
15	20	3

1951 Lionel Railroading is Fun: 17 1/4 x 23 3/4 poster printed in blue and black ink with layout ideas.

Ex	N	Rarity
10	20	4

1952 Consumer Catalog: 11 7/8 x 7 3/4, 36-page horizontal format catalog.

Ex	N	Rarity
40	55	4

1952 Lionel Railroading is Fun: 17 1/4 x 22 3/4 poster printed in orange and black ink with layout ideas.

Ex	N	Rarity
10	20	4

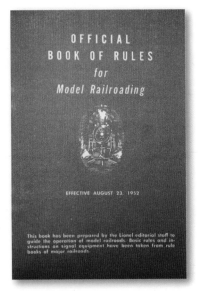

1952 Official Book of Rules for Model Railroading: 4 3/16 x 6 1/8, 16-page blue-covered booklet.

Ex	N	Rarity
15	20	4

1953 Consumer Catalog: 7 5/8 x 11 1/4, 40-page full color horizontal format catalog. Two distinctly different versions of this catalog exist, but there is no difference in value.

Ex	N	Rarity
35	60	4

1953 Miniature Catalog: 7 7/8 x 5 5/8, 32-page catalog with color cover and a mixture of color and black and white inside pages. Cover illustration duplicates that of the full-size consumer catalog.

Ex	N	Rarity
20	30	5

1953 Lionel Accessories: 9 x 6, 16-page accessory catalog printed in black and red ink.

Ex	N	Rarity
15	22	4

1954 Consumer Catalog: 11 1/4 x 7 5/8, 44-page horizontal format full-color catalog.

Ex	N	Rarity
30	45	4

1954 Miniature Catalog: 8 1/8 x 5 3/4, 32-page catalog with color cover and black and red inside pages. Cover illustration duplicates that of the full-size consumer catalog.

Ex	N	Rarity
20	30	5

1954 Lionel Accessories: 9 x 6, 20-page accessory catalog printed in black and green ink.

Ex	N	Rarity
6	10	3

1954 Distributor's Advertising Promotions: 8 3/8 x 11, 16-page
privately printed black and white catalog. Made of pulp-type paper.

Ex	N	Rarity
14	20	5

1955 Advance Catalog: Black & White Cover or Orange, black, and white cover.

Ex	N	Rarity
35	55	6

1955 Consumer Catalog: 11 1/4 x 7 5/8, 44-page full-color horizontal format catalog.

Ex	N	Rarity
25	40	3

1956 Advance Catalog: 11 x 8, 48-page horizontal format black and white catalog with red, white and black cover.

Ex	N	Rarity
60	100	7

1956 Consumer Catalog: 11 1/4 x 7 5/8, 40-page full-color horizontal format catalog.

Ex	N	Rarity
30	45	3

1956 Accessory Catalog: 11 x 8, 24-page horizontal format catalog printed in red and black on pulp paper.

Ex	N	Rarity
35	50	5

1957 Consumer Catalog: 11 1/4 x 7 1/2, 52-page full-color horizontal format catalog.

Ex	N	Rarity
20	30	4

1957 Accessory Catalog: 10 x 7 1/2, 32-page horizontal format catalog printed on pulp paper.

Ex	N	Rarity
10	15	5

1957 HO Catalog: 10 7/8 x 7 5/8, four-page color brochure.

Ex	N	Rarity
10	15	5

1958 Advance Catalog: 10 7/8 x 8 1/4, 64-page horizontal format catalog.

Ex	N	Rarity
35	60	6

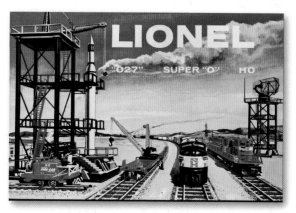

1958 Consumer Catalog: 11 1/4 x 7 5/8, 56-page full-color horizontal format catalog.

Ex	N	Rarity
18	25	4

1958 Accessory Catalog: 11 1/8 x 8, 32-page horizontal format catalog printed on pulp paper.

Ex	N	Rarity
10	15	5

1958 HO Catalog: Six-page full-color horizontal format brochure.

Ex	N	Rarity
10	15	5

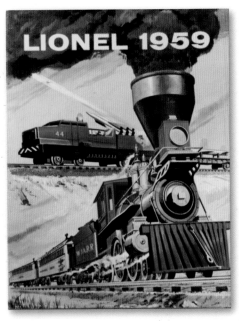

1959 Advance Catalog: 8 1/2 x 10 7/8, 44-page vertical format catalog.

Ex	N	Rarity
25	40	5

1959 Consumer Catalog: 11 x 8 1/2, 56-page full-color horizontal format catalog.

Ex	N	Rarity
18	25	4

1959 Accessory Catalog: 8 x 11, 36-page vertical format catalog printed on pulp paper.

Ex	N	Rarity
10	15	5

1960 Advance Catalog: 8 1/2 x 11, 60-page vertical format catalog.

Ex	N	Rarity
20	30	4

1960 Consumer Catalog: 8 3/8 x 11, 56-page full-color horizontal format catalog.

Ex	N	Rarity
14	20	3

1960 Accessory Catalog: 8 5/8 x 11, 36-page vertical format catalog printed on pulp paper.

Ex	N	Rarity
6	10	5

1960 HO Catalog: 8 1/2 x 10 7/8, 12-page vertical format color catalog.

Ex	N	Rarity
6	10	5

1961 Advance Catalog: 8 1/2 x 11, 76-page vertical format catalog.

Ex	N	Rarity
30	45	6

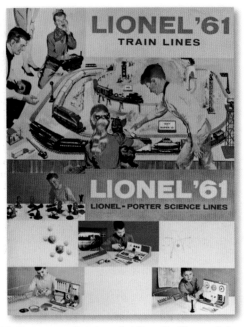

1961 Consumer Catalog: 8 1/2 x 11, 72-page full-color vertical format catalog printed on coated stock.

Ex	N	Rarity
14	20	3

1962 Advance Catalog: 8 1/2 x 11, 64-page vertical format catalog.

Ex	N	Rarity
30	45	6

1962 Lionel-Spear-Tri-ang Advance Catalog: 8 3/8 x 11, 55-page vertical format catalog.

Ex	N	Rarity
15	25	5

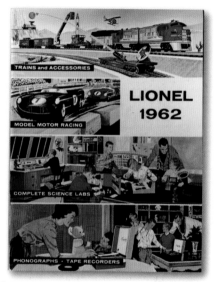

1962 Consumer Catalog: 8 1/2 x 11, 100-page full-color vertical format catalog printed on coated stock. Includes slot cars and science products.

Ex	N	Rarity
14	20	3

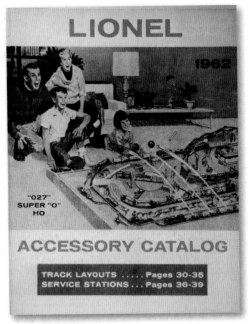

1962 Accessory Catalog: 8 3/8 x 10 7/8, 40-page vertical format catalog printed on pulp paper.

Ex	N	Rarity
6	10	5

1962 Lionel Track Layouts: 8 3/8 x 11, four-page brochure showing track layouts in 027, Super 0 and HO gauges.

Ex	N	Rarity
8	12	5

1962 Promotional Literature: 8 1/2 x 11, four-page brochure entitled "Planning Guide to Setting Up Your Lionel Trains and Accessory Department."

Ex	N	Rarity
25	40	6

1963 Advance Catalog: 8 1/2 x 11, 80-page vertical format catalog.

Ex	N	Rarity
50	85	7

1963 Consumer Catalog: 8 3/8 x 10 7/8, 56-page vertical format catalog printed with full-color cover. Includes slot cars and science products.

Ex	N	Rarity
7	12	3

1963 Science Catalog: 8 3/8 x 10 7/8, 32-page vertical format catalog printed on pulp paper.

Ex	N	Rarity
6	10	5

1964 Consumer Catalog: 8 1/2 x 11, 24-page vertical format catalog printed on coated or pulp stock.

Ex	N	Rarity
9	14	3

1965 Consumer Catalog: 8 1/2 x 10 7/8, 40-page vertical format catalog printed on coated or pulp stock. Includes slot cars and science products.

Ex	N	Rarity
11	18	3

1966 Consumer Catalog: 10 7/8 x 8 3/8, 40-page full-color horizontal format catalog.

Ex	N	Rarity
10	15	3

1968 Advance Product Sheet: A far cry from the thick advance catalogs of just a few years earlier, this single 8 1/2 x 11 white card showed in blue what was to be the 1968 product line.

Ex	N	Rarity
10	16	7

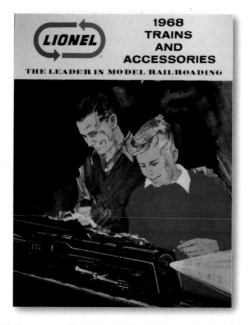

1968 Consumer Catalog: 8 1/2 x 11, 8-page vertical format full color catalog.

Ex	N	Rarity
8	12	3

HO Gauge

From 1957 through 1966, Lionel marketed HO (1/87 scale) trains in
an unsuccessful effort to gain a foothold in this growing market. Insufficient
information is available at this time to provide a scarcity rating for these products.

#	Description	EX	LN	R
0039 TRACK CLEANING CAR: 1961		70	100	200
0050 GANG CAR: 1959		60	100	200
0055 LOCOMOTIVE: 1961, M&StL switcher		50	100	200
0056 LOCOMOTIVE: 1959, A.E.C. Switcher		75	150	300
0057 LOCOMOTIVE: 1959, U.P. Switcher		50	100	200-
0058 LOCOMOTIVE: 1960, R.I. Switcher		40	80	150
0059 LOCOMOTIVE: 1960, U.S. Air Force Switcher		50	100	200
0068 INSPECTION CAR: 1961		50	100	200
0100 POWER PACK: 1961		15	20	40
0101 POWER PACK: 1961		15	20	40
0103 POWER PACK: 1959		15	20	40
0103-800 POWER PACK: 1961		15	20	40
0104 POWER PACK: 1961		15	20	40
0110 TRESTLE SET: 1958		15	20	40
0111 TRESTLE SET: 1959		15	20	40
0114 ENGINE HOUSE: 1958, w/horn		75	100	200

#	Description	VG	EX	LN
0115 KIT: 1961, engine house		52	70	150
0117 ENGINE HOUSE: 1959		68	90	175
0118 ENGINE HOUSE: 1958, with whistle		75	100	200
0119 TUNNEL: 1959		10	15	30
0140 BANJO SIGNAL: 1962		33	45	75

#	Description	VG	EX	LN
0145 GATEMAN: 1959, automatic		45	60	100
0150 RECTIFIER: 1958		3	4	10
0181 CAB CONTROL: 1958		13	25	50
0197 RADAR ANTENNA: 1958		30	40	75
0214 GIRDER BRIDGE: 1958		5	15	25
0222 DECK BRIDGE: 1961		15	20	35
0224 GIRDER BRIDGE: 1961		10	15	30
0226 TRUSS BRIDGE: 1961		10	15	30
0245-200 CONTACTOR: 1960		5	7	15
0252 CROSSING GATE: 1959		30	40	75

#	Description	VG	EX	LN
0300 LUMBER CAR: 1960, operating		15	25	50
0301 DUMP CAR: 1960, operating		20	40	75
0301-16 CARGO BIN: 1960		5	7	15
0319 HELICOPTER CAR: 1960, operating		25	50	100
0337 GIRAFFE CAR: 1961, operating		25	50	100
0349 TURBO MISSILE FIRING CAR:		50	100	200

#	Description	VG	EX	LN
0357 COP AND HOBO CAR: 1962		20	40	75
0365 MISSILE LAUNCHING CAR: 1962		30	50	100
0366 MILK CAR: 1961, operating		30	60	110
0370 SHERIFF AND OUTLAW CAR: 1962		20	40	75
0410 SUBURBAN RANCH HOUSE: 1959		15	20	45
0411 FIGURE SET: 1959		15	20	45
0412 FARM SET: 1959		15	20	45
0413 RAILROAD STRUCTURE SET: 1959		15	20	45
0414 VILLAGE SET: 1959		15	20	45

#	Description	VG	EX	LN
0425 FIGURE SET: 1962		10	15	30
0430 TREE ASSORTMENT: 1959		10	14	25
0431 LANDSCAPE SET: 1959		15	20	40
0432 TREE ASSORTMENT: 1961		10	15	30
0470 MISSILE LAUNCHING PLATFORM: 1960		40	65	125
0480 MISSILE FIRING RANGE SET: 1961		10	15	30
0500 LOCOMOTIVE: 1957, C&NW FM C-Liner powered A Unit		50	100	150

#	Description	VG	EX	LN
0501 LOCOMOTIVE: 1957, T&P FM C-Liner powered A UNIT		75	120	200
0502 LOCOMOTIVE: 1957, Wabash FM C-Liner powered A unit		30	65	125
0503 LOCOMOTIVE: 1957, WP FM C-Liner powered A unit		30	65	125
0504 LOCOMOTIVE: 1957, SP FM C-Liner powered A unit		75	120	200

#	Description	VG	EX	LN
0505 LOCOMOTIVE: 1957, IC FM C-Liner powered A unit		25	50	100
0510 LOCOMOTIVE: 1957, C&NW FM C-Liner dummy A unit		50	100	150
0511 LOCOMOTIVE: 1957, T&P FM C-Liner Dummy A Unit		30	65	125
0512 LOCOMOTIVE: 1957, Wabash FM C-Liner dummy A unit		25	50	100
0513 LOCOMOTIVE: 1957, WP FM C-Liner Dummy A unit		25	50	100
0514 LOCOMOTIVE: 1957, SP FM C-Liner Dummy A unit		50	100	150
0515 LOCOMOTIVE: 1957, IC FM C-Liner Dummy A unit		25	50	100
0520 LOCOMOTIVE: 1957, C&NW FM C-Liner Dummy B unit		50	100	150

#	Description	VG	EX	LN
0521 LOCOMOTIVE: 1957, T&P FM C-Liner Dummy B unit		30	65	125
0522 LOCOMOTIVE: 1957, Wabash FM C-Liner Dummy B unit		25	50	100
0523 LOCOMOTIVE: 1957, WP FM C-Liner Dummy B unit		25	50	100
0524 LOCOMOTIVE: 1957, SP FM C-Liner Dummy B unit		50	100	150
0525 LOCOMOTIVE: 1957, IC FM C-Liner Dummy B unit		25	50	100
0530 LOCOMOTIVE: 1958, DRGW, Diesel F-3 powered A				
0531 LOCOMOTIVE: 1958, C.M. ST. P&P, Diesel F-3 powered A		30	65	125
0532 LOCOMOTIVE: 1958, Diesel F-3 powered A, B&O		30	65	125
0533 LOCOMOTIVE: 1958, New Haven, Diesel F-3 powered A,		30	65	125
0535 LOCOMOTIVE: 1962, Santa Fe, Diesel ALCO, AB		30	65	125
0536 LOCOMOTIVE: 1963, Santa Fe, Diesel ALCO		30	65	125
0537 LOCOMOTIVE: 1966, Diesel ALCO, AB Santa Fe		30	65	125
0540 LOCOMOTIVE: 1958, DRGW, Diesel F-3, Dummy B		25	50	100
0541 LOCOMOTIVE: 1958, CMST P&P, Diesel F-3, Dummy B		25	50	100
0550 LOCOMOTIVE: 1958, DRGW, Diesel F-3, Dummy A		25	50	100
0555 LOCOMOTIVE: 1963, Santa Fe, Diesel F-3 powered A		30	65	125

#	Description	VG	EX	LN

0561 ROTARY SNOWPLOW: 1959, MSTL | 60 | 100 | 200

0564 LOCOMOTIVE: 1960, C&O, Diesel ALCO, powered A | 30 | 65 | 125

0565 LOCOMOTIVE: 1959, Santa Fe, Diesel ALCO, powered A | 30 | 65 | 125

#	Description	VG	EX	LN
0566 LOCOMOTIVE: 1959, Texas Special, Diesel ALCO, powered A		30	65	125
0567 LOCOMOTIVE: 1959, Alaska, Diesel ALCO, powered A		30	65	125
0568 LOCOMOTIVE: 1962, Union Pacific, Diesel ALCO, powered A		30	65	125
0569 LOCOMOTIVE: 1963, Union Pacific, Diesel ALCO, powered A		30	65	125
0570-1 NAVY YARD SWITCHER:		60	100	200

#	Description	VG	EX	LN
0571 LOCOMOTIVE: 1963, PRR, Diesel ALCO, powered A		30	65	125
0576 LOCOMOTIVE: 1959, Texas Special, Diesel F-3, dummy B		30	65	125
0577 LOCOMOTIVE: 1959, Alaska, Diesel F-3, dummy B		30	65	125
0581 LOCOMOTIVE: 1960, PRR, Rectifier		30	65	125

#	Description	VG	EX	LN
0586 LOCOMOTIVE: 1959, Texas Special, Diesel F-3, dummy A		25	50	100
0587 LOCOMOTIVE: 1959, Alaska, Diesel F-3, dummy A		25	50	100

0591 LOCOMOTIVE: 1959, New Haven, Rectifier	30	65	125
0592 LOCOMOTIVE: 1966, Santa Fe, Diesel GP9	30	65	125

#	Description	VG	EX	LN
0593 LOCOMOTIVE: 1963, Northern Pacific, Diesel GP9		30	65	125
0594 LOCOMOTIVE: 1963, Santa Fe, Diesel GP9		30	65	125
0595 LOCOMOTIVE: 1959, Santa Fe, Diesel F-3, dummy A		25	50	100
0596 LOCOMOTIVE: 1959, NYC, diesel GP9		30	65	125
0597 LOCOMOTIVE: 1961, Northern Pacific, Diesel GP9		30	65	125
0598 LOCOMOTIVE: 1961, NYC, diesel GP7		30	65	125
0602 0-6-0 STEAM LOCOMOTIVE: 1960		25	50	100
0605 0-4-0 TANK-TYPE STEAM LOCOMOTIVE: 1959		30	65	125
0625 4-6-2 STEAM LOCOMOTIVE: 1959		45	90	175
0626 4-6-2 STEAM LOCOMOTIVE: 1963		35	65	125
0635 4-6-2 STEAM LOCOMOTIVE: With Smoke, 1963		30	65	125

0636 4-6-2 STEAM LOCOMOTIVE: 1963		30	65	125
0637 4-6-2 STEAM LOCOMOTIVE: 1963		30	65	125

#	Description	VG	EX	LN
0642 2-4-2 STEAM LOCOMOTIVE: 1961		30	65	125
0643 2-4-2 STEAM LOCOMOTIVE: 1963		30	65	125
0645 4-6-2 STEAM LOCOMOTIVE: With Smoke, 1962		30	65	125
0646 4-6-2 STEAM LOCOMOTIVE: With Smoke, 1963		30	65	125
0647 4-6-2 STEAM LOCOMOTIVE: With Smoke, 1966		30	65	125

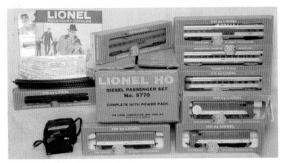

#	Description	VG	EX	LN
0704 BAGGAGE CAR: 1959, Texas Special	30	60	125
0705 PULLMAN: 1959, Texas Special	30	60	125
0706 VISTA DOME: 1959, Texas Special	30	60	125
0707 OBSERVATION CAR: 1959, Texas Special	30	60	125
0708 BAGGAGE CAR: 1960, Pennsylvania	10	20	40
0709 VISTA DOME: 1960, Pennsylvania	13	25	50
0710 OBSERVATION CAR: 1960, Pennsylvania	10	20	40

#	Description	VG	EX	LN
0711 BAGGAGE CAR: 1960, Pennsylvania		10	20	40
0712 BAGGAGE CAR: 1961, Santa Fe		25	45	100
0713 PULLMAN: 1961, Santa Fe		25	45	100
0714 VISTA DOME: 1961, Santa Fe		13	25	50
0715 OBSERVATION CAR: 1961, Santa Fe		10	20	40
0723 PULLMAN: 1963, Pennsylvania		10	20	40
0725 OBSERVATION CAR: 1963, Pennsylvania		10	20	40
0733 PULLMAN: 1964, Santa Fe		10	20	40
0735 OBSERVATION CAR: 1964, Santa Fe		10	20	40
0800 FLATCAR: 1958, with airplane		30	60	125
0801 FLATCAR: 1958, with boat		15	30	60

#	Description	VG	EX	LN
0805 AEC CAR: 1959, with light		20	40	75
0806 FLATCAR: 1959, with helicopter		25	50	100
0807 FLATCAR: 1959, with bulldozer		25	45	90

#	Description	VG	EX	LN
0808 FLATCAR: With tractor, 1959-60, red NYC		25	45	90
0809 HELIUM TRANSPORT CAR: 1961		20	35	75
0810 GENERATOR TRANSPORT CAR: 1961		15	25	50
0811-25 FLAT: 1958, with stakes		10	20	40
0813 MERCURY CAPSULE CAR: 1962		15	30	60

#	Description	VG	EX	LN
0814 AUTO TRANSPORT CAR: NYC		25	50	100
0814 AUTO TRANSPORT CAR: SP		25	50	100
0815 TANK CAR: 1958		20	35	75

#	Description	VG	EX	LN
0815-75 TANK CAR: Lionel Lines, orange, 1963 stamped 0815200		10	25	50
0815-50 TANK CAR: 1964		10	25	50
0815-85 TANK CAR: 1964		10	25	50
0815-110 SUNOCO TANK CAR: Black		65	150	350
0816-50 ROCK FUEL TANK CAR: 1962		13	25	50
0816 ROCKET FUEL TANK CAR: 1962		13	25	50
0817 CABOOSE: 1958		12	25	50
0817-250K CABOOSE: 1959, Texas Special		10	20	40
0817-300 CABOOSE: 1959, Southern Pacific		10	20	40
0817-275 CABOOSE: 1959, New Haven		10	20	40
0817-200 CABOOSE: 1959, AEC		10	20	40
0817-225 CABOOSE: 1959, Alaska		10	20	40
0817-150 CABOOSE: 1960, Santa Fe		10	20	40
0817-350 CABOOSE: 1960, Rock Island		10	20	40

#	Description	VG	EX	LN
0819-1 WORK CABOOSE: 1958, P.R.R.		13	25	50
0819-100 WORK CABOOSE: 1958, B&M		13	25	50
0819-200 WORK CABOOSE: 1959, B&M		13	25	50
0819-225 WORK CABOOSE: 1960, Santa Fe		13	25	50
0819-250 WORK CABOOSE: 1960, NP		13	25	50
0819-275 WORK CABOOSE: 1960, C&O		13	25	50
0819-285 WORK CABOOSE: 1963, C&O		13	25	50
0821 PIPE CAR: 1960		13	25	50
0821-100 PIPE CAR: 1963		15	30	65
0821-50 PIPE CAR: 1964		13	25	50
822 CABOOSE: O GA., 1915		40	75	150
0823 TWIN MISSILE CAR: 1960		35	70	150
0824 FLATCAR: 1958, with two cars		20	45	100
0827 CABOOSE: 1961, Lionel		10	20	40
0827-50 CABOOSE: 1963, AEC		10	20	40
0827-75 CABOOSE: 1963, Lionel		10	20	40
0830 FLATCAR: 1958, W/TWO VANS		20	40	75
0834 POULTRY CAR: 1959		20	40	80

# Description	VG	EX	LN
08361 HOPPER: 1959-63, Alaska, red	10	20	40
0836-100 HOPPER: 1964, Lionel	10	20	40
0836-60 HOPPER: 1966, Alaska	10	20	40
0837 CABOOSE: 1961, M&STL	8	15	30
0837-100 CABOOSE: 1963, M&STL	10	20	40
0838 CABOOSE: 1961, Lackawanna	10	20	40
0840 CABOOSE: 1961, NYC	10	20	40
0841 CABOOSE: 1961	10	20	40
0841-50 CABOOSE: 1962, Union Pacific	10	20	40
0841-175 CABOOSE: 1962, Santa Fe	10	20	40
0842 CULVERT PIPE CAR: 1960	12	25	50
0845 GOLD BULLION CAR: 1962	40	75	150
0847-100 EXPLODING TARGET CAR: 1960	30	60	125
0847 EXPLODING TARGET CAR: 1960	10	20	40
0850-100 MISSILE LAUNCHING CAR	20	40	75
0850 MISSILE LAUNCHING CAR: 1960	20	35	75
0860 DERRICK: 1958	15	30	65
0861 TIMBER TRANSPORT CAR: 1960	10	20	40
0861-100 TIMBE TRANSPORT CAR: 1961	25	50	
0862 GONDOLA: 1958	5	10	30

#	Description	VG	EX	LN
0862-200 GONDOLA: 1958		60	100	200
0863 RAIL TRUCK CAR: 1960		13	25	50
0864-175 BOXCAR: 1958, Timken		10	20	40
0864-225 BOXCAR: 1958, Central of Georgia		30	60	125
0864-25 BOXCAR: 1958, NYC		10	20	40
0864-200 BOXCAR: 1958, Monon		10	20	40
0864-250 BOXCAR: 1958, Wabash		10	20	40
0864-125 BOXCAR: 1958, Rutland		10	20	40
0864-50 BOXCAR: 1958, State of Maine		10	20	40
0864-1 BOXCAR: 1958, Seaboard		10	20	40
0864-100 BOXCAR: 1958, New Haven		10	20	40
0864-150 BOXCAR: 1958, M&STL		10	20	40
0864-900 BOXCAR: 1959, NYC		10	20	40
0864-300 BOXCAR: 1959, Alaska		10	20	40
0864-325 BOXCAR: 1959, D.S.S.A.		10	20	40
0864-350 BOXCAR: 1959, State of Maine		15	30	60
0864-400 BOXCAR: 1960, B&M		10	20	40
0864-700 BOXCAR: 1961, Santa Fe		10	20	40
0864-275 BOXCAR: 1962, State of Maine		10	20	40
0864-935 BOXCAR: 1963, NYC		10	20	40
0864-925 BOXCAR: 1964, NYC		10	20	40
0865 GONDOLA: 1958, with canisters		15	30	65
0865-225 GONDOLA: 1960, with scrap iron		13	25	50
0865-250 GONDOLA: 1960, with crates		13	25	50
0865-300 GONDOLA: 1963, with crates		13	25	50
0865-350 GONDOLA: 1963, NYC		10	20	40
0865-375 GONDOLA: 1963, NYC		10	20	40
0865-400 GONDOLA: 1963, NYC with crates		10	20	40
0865-435 GONDOLA: 1964		10	20	40

#	Description	VG	EX	LN
0866-1 CATTLE CAR: 1958, M.K.T.		10	20	40
0866-25 CATTLE CAR: 1958, Santa Fe		10	20	40
0866-200 CIRCUS CAR: 1959		15	32	65
0870 MAINTENANCE CAR: 1959, with generator		15	30	60
0872-50 REEFER: 1958, El Capitan		10	20	40
0872-25 REEFER: 1958, Illinois Central		10	20	40
0872-1 REEFER: 1958, Fruit Growers		10	20	40
0872-200 REEFER: 1959, Railway Express		10	20	40

#	Description	VG	EX	LN
0873 RODEO CAR: 1962		20	40	
0874 BOXCAR: 1964, NYC		50	100	
0874-60 BOXCAR: 1964, B&M		10	20	40
0874-25 BOXCAR: 1965, NYC		10	20	40
0875 FLATCAR: 1959, with missile		20	35	75
876 HELIOS 21 SPACESHIP: 1965		20	40	80
0877 MISCELLANEOUS CAR: 1958		10	20	40
0879 DERRICK: 1958		13	25	50
0880 MAINTENANCE CAR: 1959, with light		30	60	125

# Description	VG	EX	LN
0900 OPERATING PLATFORM: 1960	20	35	75
902-5 ROCKS: 1958	—	3	5
0903 TRACK: 1958, straight, 3"	—	—	1
0905 TRACK: 1958, straight, 1-1/2"	—	—	1
0906 TRACK: 1968, straight, 6"	—	—	1
0909 TRACK: 1958, straight, 9"	—	—	1
0922 REMOTE CONTROL SWITCH: 1958, right	2	3	5
0923 REMOTE CONTROL SWITCH: 1958, left	2	3	5
0925-10 INSULATING CLIP: 1960	—	-	1
0925 TERMINAL TRACK: 1958, straight	-	1	2
0929 UPCOUPLING TRACK: 1958, 9"	1	3	5
0930 30 DEGREES CROSSING: 1960	1	3	5
0939 UNCOUPLER: 1958	1	3	5
0942 MANUAL SWITCH: 1958, right	1	3	5
0943 MANUAL SWITCH: 1958, left	1	3	5
0950 RE-RAILER: 1958	1	3	5
0960 BUMPER TRACK: 1960	—	1	2
0961 BUMPER TRACK: 1961, illuminated	—	1	2
0975 TERMINAL TRACK: 1958, curved	1	1	2
0983 CURVED TRACK: 1958, curved, 3", 18" radius	—	—	1
0984 CURVED TRACK: 1958, 4-1/2", 18" radius	—	—	1
0985 CURVED TRACK: 1958, 9", 15" radius	—	—	1
0986 TRACK: 1958, curved, 4-1/2", 15" radius	—	—	1
0989 TRACK: 1958, curved, 9", 18" radius	—	—	1
0990 90 DEGREES CROSSING: 1958	5	7	10
5402 RAILROAD AND ROADWAY CROSSING: 1963	1	2	5

Appendix. How to Clean and Prepare Trains for Use.

In the instruction booklet Lionel furnished with its outfits in the 1950s, it recommended to customers that they keep all the original packaging materials to protect the trains during storage or travel. Oftentimes, however, that was not the case, and the boxes went outside or in the fireplace Christmas morning.

In the passing years, trains were stored in attics, basements or closets, oftentimes in no box at all. Dust and dirt filtered into the working mechanisms of the trains as well as coated the shiny finish Lionel carefully applied to their bodies. Stored in hot attics, lubricants solidified into solid blocks. In damp basements, humidity allowed rust to work its evil on plated or blackened surfaces and on wheels once worn shiny from use.

If it is your intention to sell your trains to a collector or dealer wholesale, then it is my recommendation that you do not attempt to clean the trains. The dealer or collector knows how to clean each piece without damage and can tell even in a dirty state how the item will clean up and what it will be worth. He will pay slightly less for a dirty piece to recoup his time. However, certain trains are easily damaged by inappropriate cleaning and, once the damage is done, the value is permanently diminished. Better that you allow the dealer do the clean up than for you to take this risk.

If you are keeping the trains for yourself and want to clean them up, what follows are a few general tips.

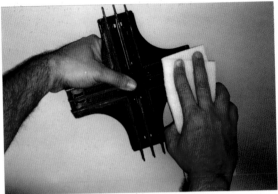

Dirty, rusty track is best cleaned by scouring with a Scotchbrite pad as seen here. Do NOT use steel wool or sandpaper.

The first thing that most people notice needs cleaning is the track. Do NOT use steel wool or sandpaper to clean the track. Steel wool will deposit fine metal fibers that will cause short circuits and sandpaper will remove the tinplating that protects the track from further rust. Excellent results can be had with 3-M "Scotchbrite" pads available in auto parts stores. Various textures are available. These non-metallic pads make short work of dirt and light rust deposits, especially the courser textures. While the entire exposed surface of the connecting pins needs to be clean, only the tops of the rails require thorough cleaning.

If the train is painted red, it is my recommendation that you do no more than dust it off. If you feel more thorough cleaning is required, consult *The Standard Catalog of Lionel Trains, 1945-69.*

Lionel's trains were well-made, reliable toys. Often they will work as well today as the day they were made. However there are some simple steps you should take to protect the trains, and more importantly you and your family, before plugging in the toys you just hauled down from the attic or home from a garage sale.

The instructions below serve two purposes. They will aid failing memories in the event the train's original instructions have been lost or discarded. They also contain some necessary tips due to the age of the trains. Remember, when Lionel wrote its instruction sheets, they were for use with new toys!

Using the pair of wire strippers (shown in Appendix 1) carefully remove a short section of the insulation from each end of the hook up wire.

First, and absolutely most importantly, examine the transformer (power pack). If it has been exposed to an obvious roof leak, or a has a broken or cracked case, take it to a qualified Lionel service man before proceeding. Next, grasp the power cord and bend it 180 degrees, tightly. If the insulation cracks or breaks off, the transformer needs service. This is a common problem, and the transformer is the only area with much potential for injury. Do not be tempted to wrap the cord in electrical tape or to splice on a new wire. Lionel knotted its power cords inside the transformer case to act as a strain relief, and the insulation there will be failing if the insulation you can see is.

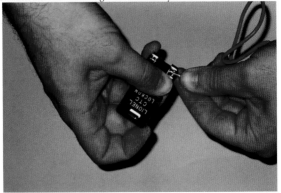

Depress the end of one fahnstock clip on the lockon and slip the end of the wire through to SMALL look. Releasing the end of the clip locks it in place. Repeat the process with the second wire and the other fahnstock clip, ensuring that not even a single strand of wire touches between the two clips.

Next, examine the visible wiring on the underside of illuminated or operating cars such as steam locomotive tenders, cabooses, passenger cars or unloading freight cars. Make sure that none of the tiny wire leads have broken loose, and that the insulation on those leads is still intact and pliable.

Should you choose to permanently attach your train's track to a board, don't do this until it has been test run, and then use screws, not nails to attach the truck. Nails work loose, and a misplaced hammer blow can permanently deform the rails. Even at this, based on the author's years of experience in the hobby shop industry, if the train is for a child, resist the urge to fasten the track to a sheet of plywood. This is, in essence, the same as gluing together Legos. The creativity, as well as the ability to expand the railroad, stops when the track is screwed down. From then on, the child is destined to only watch the train circle around a sheet of plywood, and hence will lose interest rapidly.

Unlike the CTC Lockon, which can be used only on 0 and 027 track, the UTC lockon (shown here), could also be used with prewar Standard Gauge track.

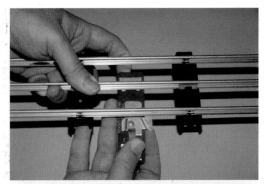

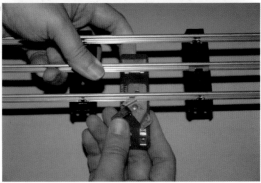

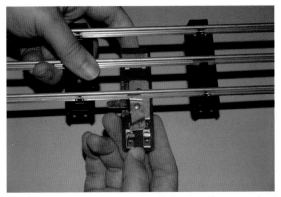

Once you have your track sections connected together, attach the wires to the end then the lockon to the track as shown in the figure here. Before placing the trains on the track, plug the transformer into a wall outlet. If your transformer is equipped with lights, the green one should now glow, and the red one, if so equipped, should be off. On transformers equipped with a red light, it indicates that the circuit breaker has opened due to a short circuit. Advance the throttle again, watching for a change in any indicator lights. A dimming green light or glowing red light is a sign of a short circuit. If your transformer has no lights, it should emit a pleasant hum when plugged in; a clicking is a sign of a short circuit.

Glossary

AAR: Association of American Railroads, an industry standards and lobbying group.

Archbar truck: Trucks constructed with side frames consisting of two strips of bar iron or steel, called Arch Bars. These bars are bent so that placed mirrored to each other they roughly form a diamond shape with extended ends. Between these ends are the axle journal boxes. These trucks were banned from interchange service in 1939.

Bakelite: A brand of hard, brittle thermoset plastic. Heating Bakelite does not soften it, making it popular for electrical components. Lionel also used Bakelite occasionally for car bodies.

Commutator: An insulated segmented copper plate connected to the coils of direct-current and universal electric motors. Current flows from the carbon brushes to the commutator segments. This allows for the reversal of current into the coils of the motor

Cupola: The raised structure on the roof of a caboose that allowed a clear view of the sides of the train, making dragging equipment and "hot boxes" easily spotted regardless of the height of the remainder of the train.

Coupler: The device for mechanically interconnecting the individual cars of a train and transmitting the draft forces. Modern railroad couplers are of the "knuckle" type, but previously link and pin as well as other types were used.

Die-casting: Manufacturing process that involves forcing molten metal, usually a zinc alloy, into a mold, called a die, under high pressure. Rugged, detailed, precisely made parts can be mass-produced in this manner.

E unit: Two meanings. A) In Lionel trains, the electromechanical switch that selects motor contacts, and thus the motor's direction of rotation, is called an "E-unit." They are usually cycled by interrupting the current flow to the track. These come in two position (forward-reverse) or three-position versions, as well as a manual version which is two position, but requires hands-on operation by the operator. Three-position E-units are the most common, and their sequence of operation is forward-neutral-reverse-neutral-forward, and so on. B) In real railroading, E-unit is slang for a General Motors Electro-Motive Division E-series twin-engine diesel that rode on two A-1-A trucks. The two terms are not generally confused as Lionel did not build a miniature E-unit during the postwar era.

Gauge: The distance between the tops of the rails. On most real U.S. railroads this is 4 feet 8 1/2 inches. For Lionel's most popular size of trains this width is 1 1/4 inches.

Heat-stamping: A decorating process whereby a heated die is used to transfer and adhere a colored decoration to the subject piece. When used on plastics, heat stamping often leaves an impression, the depth of which varies with the temperature of the tool and the duration of contact.

Hot box: Early railroad wheel bearings were lubricated with oil-soaked cotton called "waste." If the lubrication ran dry, the bearing would overheat, setting fire to the waste. If the train continued to operate, the bearing would fail, derailing the train.

House car: A term used for enclosed freight cars such as box, stock, refrigerator, and poultry cars. These cars are used for lading requiring protection from weather.

Magnetraction: This feature was intended to better keep the locomotive on the track and increase its pulling power by using powerful Alnico magnets to magnetize the wheel, "sticking" the train to Lionel's tin-plated steel track

Rubber stamping: A decorating process which uses an engraved rubber block that is inked and then pressed to.

Index